ASCENT®
CENTER FOR TECHNICAL KNOWLEDGE

Autodesk® Revit® 2021 Architecture: Conceptual Design and Visualization

Learning Guide

Metric - 1st Edition

AUTODESK.
Authorized Publisher

ASCENT - Center for Technical Knowledge®
Autodesk® Revit® 2021 Architecture:
Conceptual Design and Visualization
Metric Units - 1st Edition

Prepared and produced by:

ASCENT Center for Technical Knowledge
630 Peter Jefferson Parkway, Suite 175
Charlottesville, VA 22911

866-527-2368
www.ASCENTed.com

Lead Contributor: Cherisse Biddulph

ASCENT - Center for Technical Knowledge (a division of Rand Worldwide Inc.) is a leading developer of professional learning materials and knowledge products for engineering software applications. ASCENT specializes in designing targeted content that facilitates application-based learning with hands-on software experience. For over 25 years, ASCENT has helped users become more productive through tailored custom learning solutions.

We welcome any comments you may have regarding this guide, or any of our products. To contact us please email: feedback@ASCENTed.com.

The following are registered trademarks or trademarks of Autodesk, Inc., and/or its subsidiaries and/or affiliates in the USA and other countries: 123D, 3ds Max, ADSK, Alias, ATC, AutoCAD LT, AutoCAD, Autodesk, the Autodesk logo, Autodesk 123D, Autodesk Alias, ArtCAM, Autodesk Forge, Autodesk Fusion, Autodesk Inventor, AutoSnap, BIM 360, Buzzsaw, CADmep, CAMduct, Civil 3D, Configurator 360, Dancing Baby (image), DWF, DWG, DWG (DWG logo), DWG Extreme, DWG TrueConvert, DWG TrueView, DWGX, DXF, Eagle, , ESTmep, FBX, FeatureCAM, Flame, FormIt 360, Fusion 360, The Future of Making Things, Glue, Green Building Studio, InfraWorks, Instructables, Instructables (Instructables logo), Inventor, Inventor CAM, Inventor HSM, Inventor LT, Make Anything, Maya, Maya LT, Moldflow, MotionBuilder, Mudbox, Navisworks, Netfabb, Opticore, PartMaker, Pier 9, PowerInspect, PowerMill, PowerShape, Publisher 360, RasterDWG, RealDWG, ReCap, ReCap 360, Remake, Revit LT, Revit, Scaleform, Shotgun, Showcase, Showcase 360, SketchBook, Softimage, Tinkercad, TrustedDWG, VRED.

NASTRAN is a registered trademark of the National Aeronautics Space Administration.

All other brand names, product names, or trademarks belong to their respective holders.

General Disclaimer:

Notwithstanding any language to the contrary, nothing contained herein constitutes nor is intended to constitute an offer, inducement, promise, or contract of any kind. The data contained herein is for informational purposes only and is not represented to be error free. ASCENT, its agents and employees, expressly disclaim any liability for any damages, losses or other expenses arising in connection with the use of its materials or in connection with any failure of performance, error, omission even if ASCENT, or its representatives, are advised of the possibility of such damages, losses or other expenses. No consequential damages can be sought against ASCENT or Rand Worldwide, Inc. for the use of these materials by any third parties or for any direct or indirect result of that use.

The information contained herein is intended to be of general interest to you and is provided "as is", and it does not address the circumstances of any particular individual or entity. Nothing herein constitutes professional advice, nor does it constitute a comprehensive or complete statement of the issues discussed thereto. ASCENT does not warrant that the document or information will be error free or will meet any particular criteria of performance or quality. In particular (but without limitation) information may be rendered inaccurate by changes made to the subject of the materials (i.e. applicable software). Rand Worldwide, Inc. specifically disclaims any warranty, either expressed or implied, including the warranty of fitness for a particular purpose.

AS-RAR2101-CDV1MT-SG   //   IS-RAR2101-CDV1MT-SG

Contents

Preface

As architects and designers start a project, they frequently think about the overall massing of a building or the area of the footprint. The Autodesk® Revit® software, using its powerful Building Information Modeling (BIM) engine, includes tools for creating mass elements that can be modified into many shapes. You can then apply walls, roofs, and floors to them to continue designing. You can use space planning tools to set up areas for rooms and colors to mark the different areas. For presentations, you can create, embellish, and render perspective views.

The objective of the *Autodesk® Revit® 2021 Architecture: Conceptual Design and Visualization* guide is to enable users who have worked with the Autodesk Revit software to expand their knowledge in the area of conceptual design, including massing studies, space planning, visualization, and rendering.

Topics Covered

- Create in-place conceptual mass elements.
- Create building elements from massing studies.
- Use rooms and areas for space planning and analysis.
- Create perspectives, sketches, exploded views, and solar studies.
- Render views that include materials, lighting, and enhancements such as people and plants.

Prerequisites

- Access to the 2021.1 version of the software, to ensure compatibility with this guide. Future software updates that are released by Autodesk may include changes that are not reflected in this guide. The practices and files included with this guide might not be compatible with prior versions (e.g., 2020).
- You should be comfortable with the fundamentals of the Autodesk Revit software, as taught in the *Autodesk Revit: Fundamentals for Architecture* guide. Knowledge of basic techniques is assumed, such as creating walls, roofs, and other objects; copying and moving objects; creating and working with views; etc.
- Collaboration Tools, BIM Management, and Site and Structural Design are taught in additional guides.

Note on Software Setup

This guide assumes a standard installation of the software using the default preferences during installation. Lectures and practices use the standard software templates and default options for the Content Libraries.

Students and Educators Can Access Free Autodesk Software and Resources

Autodesk challenges you to get started with free educational licenses for professional software and creativity apps used by millions of architects, engineers, designers, and hobbyists today. Bring Autodesk software into your classroom, studio, or workshop to learn, teach, and explore real-world design challenges the way professionals do.

Get started today - register at the Autodesk Education Community and download one of the many Autodesk software applications available.

Visit www.autodesk.com/education/home/

Note: Free products are subject to the terms and conditions of the end-user license and services agreement that accompanies the software. The software is for personal use for education purposes and is not intended for classroom or lab use.

Lead Contributor: Cherisse Biddulph

Cherisse is an Autodesk Certified Professional for Revit, as well as an Autodesk Certified Instructor. She brings 15 years of industry, teaching, and technical support experience to her role as a Learning Content Developer with ASCENT. With a passion for design and architecture, she assisted several firms with CAD Manager needs and getting others up to speed on the latest software. In 2004, she joined IMAGINiT as an Application Engineer (AE), where she developed custom training and provided support for customers. She transitioned from her work as an AE to the IMAGINiT Solution Center as a Senior Technical Support Specialist, where she became proficient in AutoCAD, BIM 360, Navisworks, and Revit. Today, Cherisse continues to expand her knowledge in the ever-evolving AEC industry and the software used to support it.

Cherisse Biddulph has been the Lead Contributor for *Autodesk Revit Architecture: Conceptual Design and Visualization* since 2019.

In This Guide

The following highlights the key features of this guide.

Feature	Description
Practice Files	The Practice Files page includes a link to the practice files and instructions on how to download and install them. The practice files are required to complete the practices in this guide.
Chapters	A chapter consists of the following - Learning Objectives, Instructional Content, Practices, Chapter Review Questions, and Command Summary.
	• **Learning Objectives** define the skills you can acquire by learning the content provided in the chapter.
	• **Instructional Content**, which begins right after Learning Objectives, refers to the descriptive and procedural information related to various topics. Each main topic introduces a product feature, discusses various aspects of that feature, and provides step-by-step procedures on how to use that feature. Where relevant, examples, figures, helpful hints, and notes are provided.
	• **Practice** for a topic follows the instructional content. Practices enable you to use the software to perform a hands-on review of a topic. It is required that you download the practice files (using the link found on the Practice Files page) prior to starting the first practice.
	• **Chapter Review Questions**, located close to the end of a chapter, enable you to test your knowledge of the key concepts discussed in the chapter.
	• **Command Summary** concludes a chapter. It contains a list of the software commands that are used throughout the chapter and provides information on where the command can be found in the software.
Appendices	Appendices provide additional information to the main course content. It could be in the form of instructional content, practices, tables, projects, or skills assessment.

Practice Files

To download the practice files for this guide, use the following steps:

1. Type the URL **exactly as shown below** into the address bar of your Internet browser, to access the Course File Download page.

   Note: If you are using the ebook, you do not have to type the URL. Instead, you can access the page simply by clicking the URL below.

   ## https://www.ascented.com/getfile/id/burnettia

   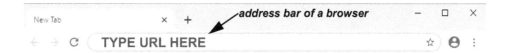

2. On the Course File Download page, click the **DOWNLOAD NOW** button, as shown below, to download the .ZIP file that contains the practice files.

3. Once the download is complete, unzip the file and extract its contents.

   The recommended practice files folder location is:
   C:\Revit 2021 Conceptual Design and Visualization Practice Files

   Note: It is recommended that you do not change the location of the practice files folder. Doing so may cause errors when completing the practices.

Stay Informed!

To receive information about upcoming events, promotional offers, and complimentary webcasts, visit:

www.ASCENTed.com/updates

Massing Studies

The Autodesk® Revit® software is a powerful tool for creating accurate building models. When you are just beginning a design, however, you do not need to have that level of accuracy and may only want to model general features, such as the overall shape of a building. The massing tools help with this initial modeling stage by enabling you to create and modify simple and complex forms directly in a project.

Learning Objectives in This Chapter

- Place and modify massing elements using existing mass families.
- Create mass forms (and void forms), including extrusions, revolves, sweeps, blends, swept blends, and lofts.
- Modify mass faces, edges, or vertices using the 3D Control feature.
- Edit profiles of mass elements.
- Add edges and profiles to mass elements.
- Divide and pattern the faces of masses.
- Create floors at selected levels in the mass.
- Add walls, roofs, curtain systems, and floors to a mass element using the Model by Face tools.

1.1 Overview of Massing Studies

When you start designing a building, you normally do not know its exact size or the locations of doors and windows. You probably do not even know what type of wall system you want to use. In some cases, you need to establish the relationship of the forms of the new building to those of the existing structures around it first, as shown in Figure 1–1. The focus is the overall shape and footprint of the building, which you develop in a massing study.

Figure 1–1

- Massing elements are intended for large forms that define the overall shape and size of a building. For smaller elements (e.g., furniture or columns), create or use family elements.

- By default, mass elements do not display in views until the Show Mass mode has been toggled on. In the *Massing & Site* tab>Conceptual Mass panel, select either:

  - (Show Mass by View Settings) - The Mass category must be toggled on in the Visibility/Graphic Overrides dialog box. Use this if you want to print or export the mass elements.

  - (Show Mass Form and Floors) - Overrides the Visibility/Graphic Overrides and toggles on mass elements and mass floors.

- **Show Mass Surface Types** and **Show Mass Zones and Shades** are connected to the subscription based Mass Analysis tools.

Premade Mass Elements

Premade mass elements (families) can be inserted into a project using the **Place Mass** command. The Autodesk® Revit® software includes several basic massing elements that work like building blocks to help you create the conceptual design, some of which are shown in Figure 1–2.

Figure 1–2

Custom Mass Elements

Custom mass elements are created in a project as an **In-Place Mass** or in a separate **Conceptual Mass** family. These families are highly customizable. They are created by drawing profiles, as shown on the left in Figure 1–3, and then applying a form, such as an extrusion (as shown on the right in Figure 1–3) or a loft.

Figure 1–3

Modifying Mass Elements

Premade mass elements can be modified using shape handles in plan, elevation, and section views, as shown in Figure 1–4. Custom mass elements can be modified using shape handles in 3D views and have additional modification options, as shown in Figure 1–5.

Figure 1–4

Figure 1–5

Making Buildings from Mass Elements

When you have finished the massing study, you can apply walls, curtain systems, roofs, and floors to the faces of the mass elements (as shown in Figure 1–6), and then proceed to the next step in the design process.

Figure 1–6

1.2 Placing Mass Elements

The most basic building blocks of massing are the mass families included with the Autodesk Revit software. These include standard building block shapes, as shown in Figure 1–7, which can be resized using shape handles in plan, elevation, and section views, and in Properties for more precise sizing. These mass families need to be loaded into a project.

If you know you are going to use these families in your massing studies, you might want to preload them into a template.

Figure 1–7

- Premade mass families are found in the Autodesk Revit Library in the *Mass* subfolder.

Hint: Family Library Location

If you do not default to the Revit family folder location, click on the **Metric Library** folder icon in the Places panel, shown in Figure 1–8 within the Open or Load Family dialog box.

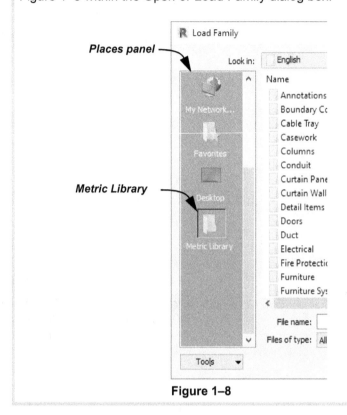

Figure 1–8

How To: Place Massing Elements

1. In the *Massing & Site* tab>Conceptual Mass panel, click

   (Place Mass).

- If you have not already toggled on Show Mass mode from the Visibility/Graphic Overrides dialog box, an alert box displays stating the program has toggled it on automatically, as shown in Figure 1–9.

Figure 1–9

- If no mass family is loaded, you are prompted to load a family, as shown in Figure 1–10. Click **Yes** to open up the Load Family dialog box.

Figure 1–10

2. In the Type Selector, select a mass type, as shown in Figure 1–11.

Figure 1–11

*Another element must be in the project for you to be able to use **Place on Face**.*

3. In the *Modify | Place Mass* tab>Placement panel, click either (Place on Face) or (Place on Work Plane). Pick a point on the screen to place the mass.

   - To rotate the mass before placing it, press <Spacebar> to rotate it in 90 degree increments.
   - To rotate the mass after you place it, select **Rotate after placement** in the Options Bar.

Modifying Basic Mass Elements

You can use Properties to modify an element's shape, material, and offset from host. You can also use shape handles to change the sizes of mass elements in plans or elevations (but not in 3D views), as shown in Figure 1–12. This method is not very precise but might be all that you need to do at this early stage of the conceptual design. The shape handle in the center flips the work plane.

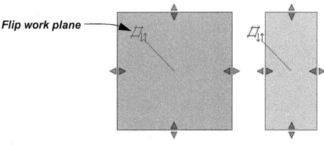

Figure 1–12

- Figure 1–13 shows the Properties for a box mass element. Dimension options vary according to the parameters of the shape.

Figure 1–13

- If you want to move an existing mass element to a different work plane, in the *Modify | Mass* tab>Work Plane panel, click

  (Edit Work Plane). Specify the new work plane in the Work Plane dialog box.

Applying Materials

The material (Default Form) for mass elements is transparent by default. Therefore, all of the edges of the mass are displayed, as shown using a Rectangle-Blended form in Figure 1–14.

Figure 1–14

- To change the material for the entire mass element, select it and in Properties, change the **Mass Material** parameter (as shown in Figure 1–15) to a different material (as shown in Figure 1–16). This only works for the standard mass elements that are included in the library.

Figure 1–15

Figure 1–16

Practice 1a | Place Mass Elements

Practice Objective

• Add mass elements using existing mass families.

In this practice, you will use basic shapes from the massing families supplied with the Autodesk Revit software to model existing buildings around a proposed site, as shown in Figure 1–17. The footprint and height for each mass are included on the toposurface.

Figure 1–17

Task 1 - Add box mass elements.

1. In the practice files folder, open **Edmon-Towers-M.rvt**.

2. Open the **Floor Plans: Existing Site** view.

3. In the *Massing & Site* tab>Conceptual Mass panel, expand

    (Show Mass by View Settings) and click (Show Mass Form and Floors).

4. In the *Massing & Site* tab>Conceptual Mass panel, click

    (Place Mass). Click **Close** if the Massing - Show Mass Enabled dialog box appears. The **M_Box** mass element family is already loaded.

5. In the *Modify | Place Mass* tab>Placement panel, verify that

    (Place on Work Plane) is selected and place several box massing elements on the site plan where you see rectangular outlines, as shown in Figure 1–18.

Figure 1–18

6. Select each box and use shape handles to resize them to fit the outline. For the angled sketches, rotate or align the boxes first. When you drag the shape handles, they automatically snap to nearby elements, as shown in Figure 1–19.

7. Use Properties to set the heights as indicated on the existing site plan, as shown in Figure 1–20.

Figure 1–19   **Figure 1–20**

8. Repeat the process to add box mass elements to the rectangular sketches in the lower right side of the site.

9. Save the project.

Task 2 - Load and add other mass elements.

1. Click (Place Mass). In the *Place | Mass* tab>Mode panel, click (Load Family).

2. In the Autodesk Revit Library, navigate to the *Mass* folder, select **M_Barrel Vault.rfa** and **M_Cylinder.rfa**, and click **Open**.

3. In the Type Selector, select **M_Cylinder**.

4. Click (Place on Work Plane), then to position the Cylinder masses at the center of the existing circles, enter **SC** (Snap Center) and select the edge of the circle to place it. Place the Cylinder mass on the three circles.

5. Change the radius by stretching the grips and heights to match the plan, as shown in Figure 1–21.

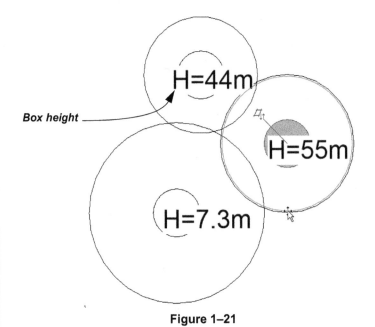

Figure 1–21

If greater accuracy is required, an in-place mass could be created to match the building footprint. For this practice, use two boxes.

6. For the angled building, use two box masses to create the base building, as shown in Figure 1–22. The two masses need to overlap slightly. Set the height of both of them as shown in the plan view.

Figure 1–22

7. Add two barrel vault mass elements using (Place on Face) to place them on the top of the box elements. Align them and then use shape handles to position them, as shown in Figure 1–23.

Figure 1–23

8. View the project in 3D.

9. Save the project.

1.3 Creating Conceptual Massing

To create custom massing elements, you need to start with an in-place mass where you can create a 3D form from 2D sketches. Masses can be made up of solid and void forms, as shown in Figure 1–24.

If you want to use a massing element more than once in a project, you should create a separate mass family.

Figure 1–24

Forms are created from a mixture of profiles, paths, and points. For example, one profile becomes an extrusion, as shown in Figure 1–25, while a profile, a point, and path, become a sweep, as shown in Figure 1–26.

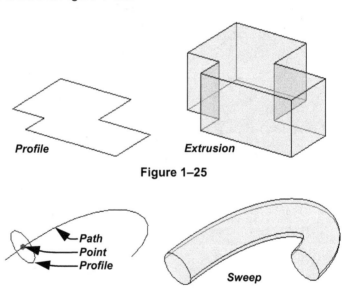

Figure 1–25

Figure 1–26

How To: Create an In-Place Mass (Overview)

1. In a project, in the *Massing & Site* tab>Conceptual Mass panel, click ⬚ (In-Place Mass).

2. In the Name dialog box, set a new name for the mass.

3. In the *Create* tab>Draw panel, click 🖊 (Model) and use the draw tools to sketch the profiles, paths, and points that make up the form.

   - Use 🖊 (Reference Line) or ✎ (Reference Plane) as guidelines to help you draw the sketches.

4. Select the profile as well as any related path or points.

   - For the profile, ensure that you select the chain of lines, as shown in Figure 1–27, instead of individual sketch lines, as shown in Figure 1–28

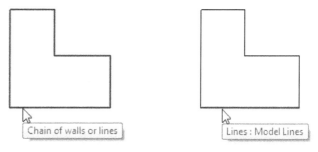

| Figure 1–27 | Figure 1–28 |

5. In the *Modify | Lines* tab>Form panel, expand 🗇 (Create Form) and select ⬓ (Solid Form) or ⬔ (Void Form).

   - A closed profile becomes a solid and an open profile becomes a surface, as shown in Figure 1–29.

Figure 1–29

6. Click ✔ (Finish Mass).

Types of Forms

Six different types of forms can be created, as shown in Figure 1–30.

Figure 1–30

Extrusions

An extrusion pushes a single profile in one direction. Although the default extrusion height is preset, you can modify it using the 3D control or temporary dimensions in a 3D view, as shown in Figure 1–31.

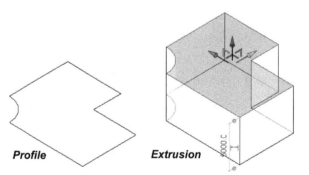

Figure 1–31

- Some profile shapes, such as a circle, have options for the shape of the form. Select the shape from the options displayed on the screen, as shown in Figure 1–32.

Figure 1–32

Blends

A blend links two profiles together. It is similar to an extrusion but is created when you select two profiles in different planes, as shown in Figure 1–33.

Figure 1–33

Lofts

A loft connects multiple profiles that do not need to be on parallel planes.It is created when you select more than two profiles in different planes, as shown in Figure 1–34.

Figure 1–34

Revolves

A revolve rotates a profile about an axis. It is created when you select an axis and a profile that are both in the same plane, as shown in Figure 1–35.

Figure 1–35

- When the axis is away from the profile, a hole is generated in the center of the revolve. To create an entirely closed shape, use a reference line for the axis, as shown in Figure 1–36.

- By default, a full circle form is created. To change this, you can select the start edge of the profile, as shown in Figure 1–36, and use the gold arrows to open it, as shown in Figure 1–37.

Figure 1–36   Figure 1–37

- You can also modify the *Start Angle* and *End Angle* in Properties, as shown in Figure 1–38.

Figure 1–38

Sweeps and Swept Blends

A sweep extends a profile along a path. It is created when you select a path and a profile, as shown in Figure 1–39. The point element defines the location of the profile on the path.

Figure 1–39

A swept blend connects two profiles along a path. It is created when you select a path connecting two profiles in different planes, as shown in Figure 1–40.

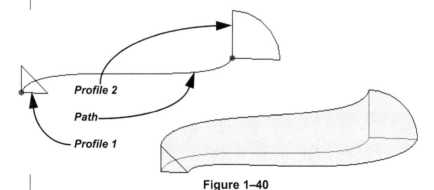

Figure 1–40

How To: Create Sweeps and Swept Blends

1. In the *Modify | Place Lines* tab>Draw panel, click

   ⌐⌐ (Model).
2. Use the drawing tools to sketch a path for the sweep to follow.

   - A single-segment path can be used with an open or closed profile. A multi-segment path requires a closed profile.
   - A swept blend can only be made from a single-segment path but you can use arcs and splines to create it.

3. In the Draw panel, click ⊙ (Point Element) and click on the path.

   - For a sweep, place a point at one end of the path.
   - For a swept blend, place a point at each end of the path.
4. Open a 3D view if you are not already in one.

5. Click ⌖ (Modify) and select the point element. A reference plane perpendicular to the path is displayed. It becomes the work plane on which you can draw the profile for a sweep, as shown in Figure 1–41.

Figure 1–41

6. Use the drawing tools to sketch a profile on the new reference plane.
7. For a swept blend, repeat the process of drawing a profile on the other end of the path.

8. Click ⌖ (Modify) and select both the path and the profile(s).
9. In the *Modify | Multi-select* or *Lines* tab>Form panel, click

   ⬡ (Create Form).

Void Forms

The process of creating void forms is essentially the same as the one for creating solid forms. The only difference is that void forms are designed to be inside a solid form so that it has a solid element to cut out, as shown in Figure 1–42.

Figure 1–42

You can change a form from solid to void. Select the solid form and in Properties in the *Identity Data* area, change the *Solid/Void* parameter, as shown in Figure 1–43.

This change can only be done to in-place mass forms.

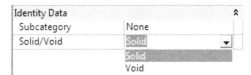

Figure 1–43

Hint: Cutting Solid Forms with Other Solid Forms

If you have two solid forms that overlap, you can use ⬚ (Cut Geometry) to cut out one of the forms, as shown in Figure 1–44.

Before cut   **After cut**

Figure 1–44

- The first form selected is cut and the second form selected remains as is.

1.4 Setting the Work Plane

Profiles and paths are the building blocks of the mass form elements. They are sketched on the current work plane which can be a face, as shown in Figure 1–45, or a specified work plane, as shown in Figure 1–46.

Figure 1–45

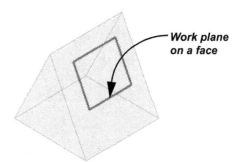

Figure 1–46

- If you are in a plan view, the related level is the active work plane by default.

How To: Establish a Work Plane by Face

1. In the *Create* tab>Draw panel, select a sketching tool.

2. In the *Modify | Place Lines* tab>Draw panel, click ✎ (Draw on Face). This is typically selected by default.

3. Hover the cursor over the face of an existing element. It highlights and you can then draw the sketch, as shown in Figure 1–47.

Sketches can be locked to faces.

Press <Tab> to cycle through nearby faces.

Work plane on a face

Figure 1–47

4. You can move directly to another face and continue drawing sketches.

How To: Establish a Work Plane by Placement Plane

1. In the *Create* tab>Draw panel, select a sketching tool. The active work plane displays with a heavy outline.

To display the work plane in a view, in the Work Plane panel, click

 (Show).

2. In the *Modify | Place Lines* tab>Draw panel, click (Draw on Work Plane).

3. In the Options Bar, in the *Placement Plane* drop-down list, select a *Level* or named reference plane, as shown in Figure 1–48.

Figure 1–48

- This list varies according to the elements contained in the massing study.

4. Draw the sketch on the plane, as shown in Figure 1–49.

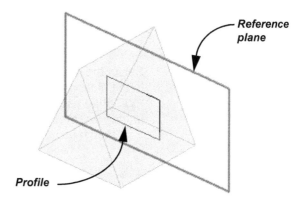

Figure 1–49

- If you have used the **Pick...** option, the selected face becomes the active work plane.

Hint: Naming Reference Planes

You can name reference planes so that they can be specified as a work plane. Select the reference plane and *<Click to name>* or in Properties, set a *Name*, as shown in Figure 1–50.

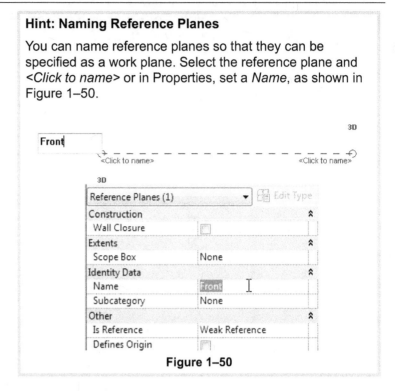

Figure 1–50

How To: Change the Work Plane of a Sketch or Form

1. Select the sketch or form.
2. In the Options Bar, click **Show Host**. The host work plane highlights, as shown in Figure 1–51.
3. In the Host drop-down list, select a new host for the sketch. The sketch moves to the selected plane.

Figure 1–51

Practice 1b | Create Mass Forms

Practice Objectives

- Create an extruded mass form.
- Create a lofted mass form.
- Add a swept void form.

In this practice, you will create two towers in a massing study. For one building, you will extrude a mass form using a simple profile. For the other building, you will create a lofted form using a variety of profiles at different levels and then add a void form using a swept profile, as shown in Figure 1–52.

Figure 1–52

Task 1 - Create an extruded in-place mass.

1. In the practice files folder, open **Edmon-Towers-New-M.rvt**.

2. Open the **Floor Plans: New Site** view. This view displays the new site area, as shown in Figure 1–53.

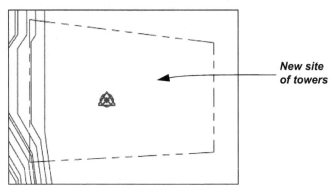

Figure 1–53

3. In the *Massing & Site* tab>Conceptual Mass panel, click

   (In-Place Mass). Click **Close** if the Massing - Show Mass Enabled dialog box appears.

4. In the Name dialog box, enter **Tower-1** and click **OK**.

Add reference planes first, if needed.

5. In the *Create* tab>Draw panel, click (Model) and then

   click (Line). Note that when you hover the cursor over the lines on the active work plane, they highlight.

6. In the northwest quadrant of the new site, draw a trapezoid shape that is roughly **24 x 18 meters**, as shown in Figure 1–54.

Figure 1–54

7. Open the default 3D view.

8. Select the lines. In the *Modify | Lines* tab>Form panel, click

   (Create Form). The Autodesk Revit software extrudes the profile to create a solid form.

9. In the 3D view, select the blue temporary dimension and change it to **42 meters**.

10. In the *Modify | Form* tab>In-Place Editor panel, click

   (Finish Mass).

Task 2 - Create levels.

1. Open the **Elevations (Building Elevation): East** view and zoom in to see the level markers.

2. Set the *elevation* of **Level 2** to **5.5 meters**.

3. Set the *name* of the existing **Roof** level to **Level 3**, and its *elevation* to **9 meters**. Click **Yes** when prompted to rename any corresponding views.

4. Select the newly named **Level 3**.

5. In the *Modify | Levels* tab>Modify panel, click ⊞ (Array). In the Options Bar, clear the **Group and Associate** option.

6. Create an array of **30 levels**, **3.5 meters** apart.

7. Click ⟍ (Modify) and enter **ZE** to zoom out to the extents of the view.

Task 3 - Create a lofted in-place mass.

1. Return to a 3D view.

2. Create a new in-place mass named **Tower-2**.

3. In the *Create* tab>Draw panel, click ⎁ (Model) and then click ⬚ (Rectangle).

4. In the Draw panel, click ⬦ (Draw on Work Plane).

5. In the Options Bar, verify that *Placement Plane* is set to **Level: Level 1**.

6. Draw a **12 x 24 meter** rectangle south of the first tower.

7. You will now draw another rectangle but this time, from the Options Bar, change *Placement Plane* to **Level: Level 10**. Vary the size of the rectangle.

8. Use the alignment lines to line up at least one of the sides with the rectangle below. Note that when you hover the cursor over the lines on the active work plane, the lines on the existing model lines highlight, as shown in Figure 1–55. (Visibility was set to Hidden Line to show the alignment line in the image below).

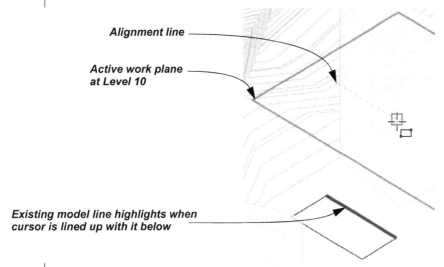

Alignment line

Active work plane
at Level 10

Existing model line highlights when
cursor is lined up with it below

Figure 1–55

9. Repeat the process at **Level 20** and **Level 30**, varying the size at each level.

10. Click (Modify) and select the four rectangles.

11. In the *Modify | Lines* tab>Form panel, click (Create Form). The new tower displays as shown in Figure 1–56. Your design will vary according to the profiles you drew.

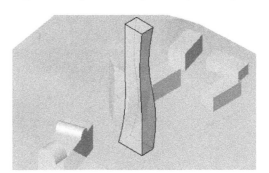

Figure 1–56

12. In **Floor Plans: Level 1** view, move one or both of the new massing forms so they do not overlap, if needed.

13. Do not click finish mass or save the project yet because you want to remain in the same in-place mass element.

Task 4 - Add a void form.

1. In a 3D view, zoom in to the base of the new tower.

2. Click 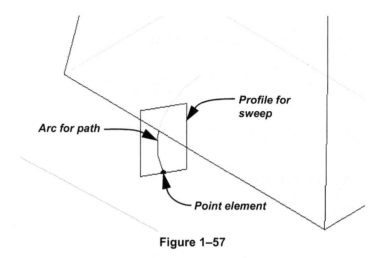 (Model) and then select one of the arc drawing tools. In the Options Bar, set the *Placement Plane* to **Level: Level 1**.

3. Draw an arc, as shown in Figure 1–57. This is the path for a sweep. It needs to start outside the existing mass to create the expected void form.

Profile for sweep

Arc for path

Point element

Figure 1–57

4. In the Draw panel, click ⊙ (Point Element).

5. Add a point at one end of the arc if you want to draw a sweep, and at both ends of the arc if you want to draw a swept blend.

6. Click (Modify) and select the point element. The Reference Point Face will highlight, as shown in Figure 1–58. This switches your work plane so you can draw your profile.

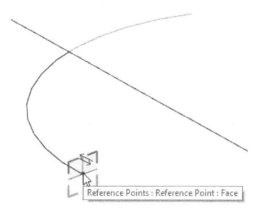

Reference Points : Reference Point : Face

Figure 1–58

7. Use Model lines to draw the profile for the sweep.

8. Repeat the process with the other point element if you are creating a swept blend.

9. Click ⟍ (Modify) and select the path and profile(s).

10. In the Form panel, expand ⊟ (Create Form) and click ⌂ (Void Form).

The new void form is cut out of the existing solid form, as shown in Figure 1–59.

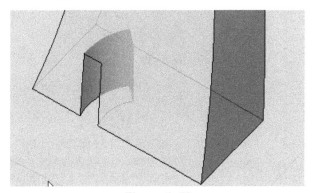

Figure 1–59

11. Click ⟍ (Finish Mass).

12. Zoom out to see the entire site with the new towers.

13. Save and close the project.

1.5 Dynamic Editing for Conceptual Massing

When a completed in-place mass element is selected, you can modify the length of its faces by dragging the controls, as shown in Figure 1–60. However, for more precise modification, you can edit the mass in-place, as shown in Figure 1–61.

Figure 1–60

Figure 1–61

- Double-click on an in-place mass, or select it and in the

  Modify | Mass tab>Model panel, click ⬚ (Edit In-Place).

In the Edit In-Place mode, you have direct access to the surface, edges, and vertices of a solid or void form, as shown in Figure 1–62. You can quickly and easily manipulate these sub-elements and create new edges and profiles.

Figure 1–62

- Press <Tab> to cycle between sub-elements to select the right one.

Using the 3D Control

When a face, edge, or vertex is selected, the 3D control is displayed.

- To move a selected sub-element directly along an axis, select one of the arrows and drag it in the appropriate direction, as shown in Figure 1–63.

- To move a selected sub-element along a plane (as shown in Figure 1–64), click and drag the plane indicator.

Figure 1–63

Figure 1–64

Other Modification Options

- You can use ✛ (Move) and ↻ (Rotate) when you select a face, an edge, or a vertex. In the example shown in Figure 1–65, the face has been rotated.

Figure 1–65

- To remove a face, an edge, or a vertex, select it and click

  ✕ (Delete), or press <Delete>. In the example shown in Figure 1–66, a vertex has been selected and deleted.

Form : Form Element : Vertex

Figure 1–66

- You can lock a mass element so that the profiles in a form work together rather than separately. Select at least one part of the form and, in the *Modify | Form* tab>Form Element panel, click ⬚ (Lock Profiles).

- When you select an edge and the form is not locked, only the selected edge moves, as shown in Figure 1–67. If you lock the form and move the same edge, the entire form based on that profile moves, as shown in Figure 1–68.

Figure 1–67   **Figure 1–68**

- To return the form to its component parts, select the mass element, and in the *Modify | Form* tab>Form Element panel, click ⬚ (Dissolve). Once you have done this, remake the entire form again.

Hint: Use X-Ray to Display a Form's Geometric Framework

Vertices, profiles, and paths do not automatically display while editing forms. In X-Ray mode, the surfaces of a form are transparent and all of the key geometric datums display, as shown in Figure 1–69.

- To enable X-Ray mode, first select a form. Note that you might need to hover the cursor over the edge and press <Tab> until a form has been highlighted. With the form selected, in the *Modify | Form* tab>Form Element panel, click (X-Ray).

Figure 1–69

- To toggle off X-Ray mode, select the form again and click (X-Ray).

- Only one form can have X-Ray mode on at a time.

1.6 Working with Profiles and Edges

While a lot can be done to manipulate mass elements using the dynamic editing tools, there are some additional commands where you can do more precise and complex editing, as shown in Figure 1–70. These include editing and adding a profile, adding edges, dividing surfaces, and splitting faces.

Figure 1–70

Editing Profiles

Form profiles are the basic shape that make up a form's geometry. While in Edit mode, you can edit the profile or path of a swept form, depending on which edge you selected before starting the editing process. For example, you can edit the profile of the bottom outline of an extruded form, as shown in Figure 1–71.

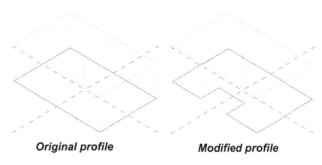

Original profile   *Modified profile*

Figure 1–71

How To: Edit Profiles

1. Double-click on the form to enter Edit mode or select the form and in the *Modify |Mass* tab>Model panel, click 🔲 (Edit In-Place).
2. Select the form or any part of the form and in the *Modify | Form* tab>Mode panel, click 🔲 (Edit Profile).
3. Pick any profile or path to edit.
4. Sketch mode opens with the profile or path highlighted in magenta. Using the **Draw** and **Modify** tools, make changes.
5. Click ✔ (Finish Edit Mode).
6. The selected profile or path is modified.
7. Click ✔ (Finish Mass).

Adding Edges and Profiles

You can also add edges and profiles to existing forms and then modify the resulting edges, faces, and vertices. An edge can be added to the sides of a form, while a profile can be added along the path of the profile, as shown in Figure 1–72.

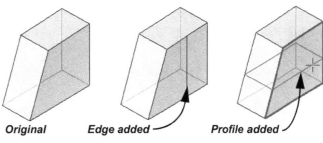

Original   *Edge added*   *Profile added*

Figure 1–72

Once the edge or profile is placed, you can use the 3D control to create new shapes, as shown in Figure 1–73.

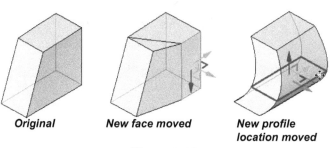

Original   New face moved   New profile location moved

Figure 1–73

- If you cannot add an edge to a face, ⊘ displays, as shown in Figure 1–74.

You cannot add an edge to the face that is parallel to the sweep path.

Figure 1–74

How To: Add an Edge

1. While in Edit mode, select anywhere on the form.
2. In the *Modify | Form* tab>Form Element panel, click ⬚ (Add Edge) or right-click and select **Add Edge**.
3. Hover the cursor over a face. A new edge that reflects the geometry displays, as shown in Figure 1–75. Alternately, pick two points at the vertices or edges of a face, as shown in Figure 1–76.

Figure 1–75

Figure 1–76

How To: Add a Profile

1. While in Edit mode, select anywhere on the form.
2. In the *Modify | Form* tab>Form Element panel, click 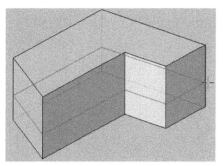 (Add Profile) or right-click and select **Add Profile**.
3. A new profile displays on the selected form when the cursor is moved onto and follows it.

    • The profile automatically adjusts its shape to match the exterior of the form wherever the cursor is located, as shown in Figure 1–77.

Figure 1–77

4. Click to place the new profile.

Modifying the Faces of Mass Elements

Mass faces can be modified to show patterns and materials. You can apply a pattern similar to creating a curtain wall layout using the **Divide Surface** option, as shown on the top of the mass element in Figure 1–78. You can also split a face into separate surfaces so you can apply different materials to each part, as shown on the base of the mass element in Figure 1–78.

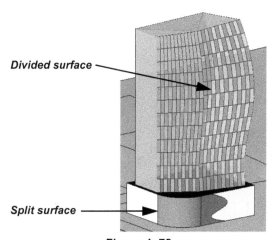

Divided surface

Split surface

Figure 1–78

How To: Divide and Pattern a Mass Face

1. Double-click on the form to enter Edit mode or select the form and in the *Modify |Mass* tab>Model panel, click (Edit In-Place).
2. Select the face of a mass element.
3. In the *Modify | Form* tab>Divide panel, click (Divide Surface).
4. The surface is divided using a basic U-V Grid, as shown in Figure 1–79.

Divided Surface : _No Pattern : _No Pattern

Figure 1–79

5. In the Type Selector, select a pattern from the patterns available, as shown in Figure 1–80.
6. In the Options Bar or Properties (as shown in Figure 1–81), modify the U-V Grid layout.

Figure 1–80

Figure 1–81

7. In the *Modify | Divide Surface* tab>contextual panels (shown in Figure 1–82), you can further modify and display the patterns.

Figure 1–82

How To: Split Mass Faces

1. In the *Modify* tab>Geometry panel, click (Split Face).
2. Select the face of the mass element you want to modify.
3. In the *Modify* tab>Draw panel, use the sketch tools to create a sketch as required, to define the split (as shown in Figure 1–83).

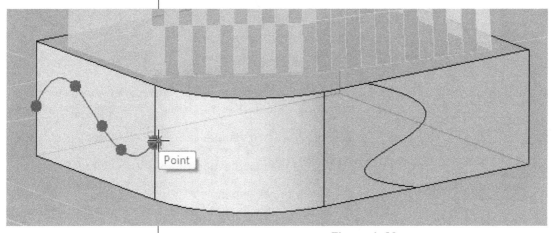

Figure 1–83

- Splitting faces does not create an additional face but you can modify the material in each area.

- The sketch that defines the split must be a closed shape completely inside the face or an open shape that touches the face edges.

- You can split the face of an in-place mass either directly on the face (without entering the mass) or in the In-Place Edit mode.

How To: Add Materials to Individual Mass Faces

1. In the *Modify* tab>Geometry panel, click (Paint).
2. Select a material in the Material Browser, as shown on the left in Figure 1–84.
   - Use the search at the top of the dialog box to narrow down your search for materials.
3. Select the face(s) of the mass that you want to paint, as shown on the right in Figure 1–84.

Search →

Figure 1–84

- Some material patterns display as shaded when you zoom out. Zoom in to display the pattern. Other material patterns only display when you are in the (Realistic) visual styles.

- To change the material applied to a face, in the *Modify* tab> Geometry panel, expand (Paint) and click (Remove Paint). Select the face(s) from which you want to remove the material.

- Older versions of materials may need to be updated with appearance assets. All legacy materials still work but they may not be as complex and nuanced when rendering.

Practice 1c | Modify In-Place Masses

Practice Objectives

- Modify mass elements.
- Add new profiles and edges.
- Modify faces by dividing or splitting them.

In this practice, you will manipulate the vertices, faces, and edges of an extruded in-place mass element using the 3D control. You will also add profiles and an edge. An example of a possible outcome is shown in Figure 1–85. Additionally, you will divide a face, apply a pattern, split another face, and then paint them with a material.

Figure 1–85

Task 1 - Modify an in-place mass.

1. In the practice files folder, open **Edmon-Towers-Modify-M.rvt**. You should be in the **3D Views: {3D View}**.

2. Select the tall mass **Tower-2** and temporarily hide the element.

3. Orient the 3D view so you can see the **Tower-1** extruded mass element.

4. Click on the mass element and modify it slightly using the controls, as shown in Figure 1–86. You can make minor modifications to an in-place mass without editing the entire mass form.

Figure 1–86

5. With the mass still selected, in the *Modify | Mass* tab>Model panel, click ⬚ (Edit In-Place).

6. Select one of the edges and modify it slightly using the 3D control, similar to that shown in Figure 1–87.

Figure 1–87

Task 2 - Add and modify profiles and an edge.

1. Select an edge in the form. (It does not matter which edge.)

2. In the *Modify | Form* tab>Form Element panel, click ⌂ (X-Ray).

3. In the Form Element panel, click ⌂ (Add Profile).

4. Add a profile about one quarter of the way up the form and press <Enter> to restart the **Add Profile** command again.

5. Add two more profiles, so that the form is divided into four sections, as shown in Figure 1–88.

Do not worry about placing the profiles exactly. Their locations can be adjusted later.

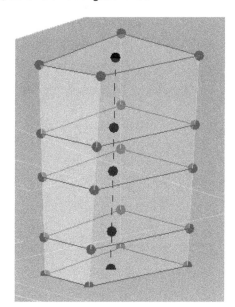

Figure 1–88

6. In the *Modify | Form* tab>Form Element panel, click ⌂ (Add Edge) to add an edge to one side of the building.

7. Click ⌖ (Modify) to exit the Add Edge command.

8. Select the new face and move it out sightly using the 3D control.

9. Manipulate the various vertices and edges to reshape the mass.

10. Toggle off X-ray mode but continue modifying the mass.

Task 3 - Divide and pattern surfaces.

1. Select one of the mass faces.

2. In the *Modify | Form* tab>Divide panel, click (Divide Surface)

3. From Properties, in the Type Selector, select a pattern.

4. Modify the pattern properties using tools in the ribbon and Options bar.

5. (Optional) Select a different face and in the *Modify | Form* tab>Geometry panel, use (Split Face) and (Paint) to apply materials.

6. Click (Finish Mass).

7. Save and close the project.

1.7 Moving from Massing to Building

When you have established a massing study, you can start the design development with walls, etc., you do not have to start over. Instead, you can use tools in the Autodesk Revit software to create walls, floors, roofs, and curtain systems from the faces of the masses in the project as shown in Figure 1–89.

Figure 1–89

- You can add a slope to a wall style from the wall's Properties, but you can also do this with mass elements by creating the shape you want and applying the material or wall style to the mass.

- You can add walls, floors, roofs, and curtain systems to the faces of mass elements using the **Wall**, **Roof**, and **Floor** commands in the *Architecture* tab>Build panel. For example, when you start the **Wall** command, you can click ▦ (Pick Faces) as the drawing method, as shown in Figure 1–90.

Figure 1–90

- You can also use the specific commands found in the *Massing & Site* tab>Model by Face panel, as shown in Figure 1–91.

Figure 1–91

How To: Use the Model by Face Tools

1. Open a view where the mass faces display and where you want to apply the building elements. This can be done in either a 3D or elevation view.

2. In the *Massing & Site* tab>Model by Face panel, click (Curtain System), (Roof), (Wall), or (Floor).

3. In the Type Selector, select an element type.
4. Select the faces you want to turn into elements.
5. In the contextual tab>Multiple Selection panel, click the related **Create** command.

Wall by Face Options

Location Line is grayed out if a curtain wall style is selected.

- Ensure that the *Location Line value* is set to **Finished Face: Exterior**. This keeps the walls on the inside of the mass.

- You can create walls on sloped faces using this tool.

Curtain Systems Options

A Curtain System is a type of curtain wall that is typically on a curved or angled face.

- In the *Modify | Place Curtain System by Face* tab>Multiple Selection panel, verify that (Select Multiple) is highlighted if you are planning to select more than one face for a curtain system at a time.

Roof by Face Options

- In the *Modify | Place Roof by Face* tab, hover over the surface so the entire face highlights, then click to place.

- In Properties, set the Constraints *Picked Faces Location* to **Faces at Bottom of the Roof**.

- From the *Modify | Place Roof by Face* tab>Multiple Selection panel, click ⬚ (Create Roof) to place your roof.

- After you have created a roof by face, you can use shape handles to modify the overhang of the roof, as shown in Figure 1–92.

The overhang distance is remembered if you change the mass.

Figure 1–92

Creating Floors from Mass Elements

To create floors in a massing study, you must first create mass floors. These are the basis for creating floors and also help track the floor area of the building. Once you have the mass floors in a project, you can click ⬚ (Floor by Face) to add the floor elements on the faces.

How To: Create Mass Floors

1. Select a mass.
2. In the *Modify | Mass* tab>Model panel, click ⬚ (Mass Floors).

3. In the Mass Floors dialog box, select the levels where you want floor area faces to be located, as shown in Figure 1–93, and click **OK**.

If you have a lot of levels to select, hold <Ctrl> or <Shift> to select multiple levels.

Figure 1–93

The mass floors display in the massing study, as shown in Figure 1–94.

Figure 1–94

- Mass floors keep track of the area, exterior surface area, volume, and perimeter of each floor. This information can be used in schedules and tags.

Hint: Updating Elements Connected to Mass Elements

Elements applied to mass elements, such as walls, floors, roofs, and curtain systems do not automatically update when the massing element changes as shown on the left in Figure 1–95. Select the mass element and in the *Modify | Mass* tab>Model panel, click ⬚ (Related Hosts). Then in the *Modify | Multi-Select* tab>Model by Face panel, click

⬚ (Update to Face). The elements update, as shown on the right in Figure 1–95.

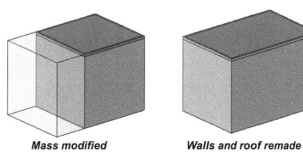

Mass modified   **Walls and roof remade**

Figure 1–95

- If you only want to update one element (such as a roof), select the element that is hosted by the mass and in the *Modify | <element type>* tab>Model by Face panel, click

  ⬚ (Update to Face). Note that the icon varies according to the element type selected.

Practice 1d

Move from Massing to Building

Practice Objectives

- Add mass floors.
- Use existing schedules to track the coverage of the site and the gross area of the mass, while making changes to one of the towers.
- Add walls, floors, roofs, and curtain systems to the finished mass towers.

In this practice, you will add mass floors to specified levels and investigate the site coverage and building volume, as shown in Figure 1–96. You will also add walls, floors, curtain systems, and roofs to the faces of the conceptual mass elements.

Figure 1–96

Task 1 - Add massing floors.

1. In the practice files folder, open **Edmon-Towers-Building-M.rvt**.

2. Select the two curved masses included in the project.

3. In the *Modify | Mass* tab>Model panel, click 🗄 (Mass Floors).

4. Select all of the levels in the Mass Floors dialog box and click **OK**. The new mass floors display as shown in Figure 1–97. Hint: Use <Shift> to select all the levels, then check one check box to check them all.

Some levels are higher than the current height of the masses. By selecting them now, they will automatically be applied when the height of the masses is changed.

Figure 1–97

Task 2 - Track site coverage and gross area using schedules.

---

1. If necessary, close any other projects and in the Quick Access Toolbar, click (Close Hidden) to close any windows that do no need to be open.

2. Open the following four views on your screen:
    *   *3D Views:* **Site View**
    *   *Floor Plans:* **New Site**
    *   *Schedules/Quantities:* **Building Volume Schedule**
    *   *Schedules/Quantities:* **Coverage of Site**

*   The **Coverage of Site** schedule enables you to track how much of the site that the proposed building covers. It lists the actual and maximum footprints in both square feet and percentage. You can enter the actual site area in the *Parcel* column and the amount of the site that the building is permitted to cover in the *Max Footprint (%)* column. The Autodesk Revit software does the rest.

*   **Building Volume Schedule** displays the Total Floor Area and Total Floor Volume at the bottom of the schedule. If the zoning restrictions or program requirements limit the overall floor area of the building, the schedule tracks this for you.

3. Return to the **3D Views:Site View** and type **WT** (Window Tile) so that all four views display.

4. Type **ZA** (Zoom All) to display the entire 3D view and the New Site plan.

5. Click in the **New Site** view and select the Property Line, as shown in Figure 1–98.

Figure 1–98

6. In Properties, the *Area* is **4022.587 m²**. This is the size you use for the *Parcel* column.

7. In the **Coverage of Site** schedule, enter **4023** in the *Parcel* cell and **20** in the *Max Footprint (%)* cell, as shown in Figure 1–99.

<Coverage of Site>				
A	B	C	D	E
Parcel	Actual Footprint	Max Footprint	Current Footprint (%)	Max Footprint (%)
4,023 m²	768 m²	865	19.1	20

Figure 1–99

8. Based on initial numbers in the **Coverage of Site** schedule, both towers are within the *Max Footprint*.

9. Select one of the tower masses. Use the shape handles to change the height and shape of the mass. Watch the schedules to ensure that the *Current Footprint* value remains below 20% and the **Building Volume schedule** *Floor Area* total remains below **16,000 m²**.

10. If you have time, you can also modify the masses using **Edit In-Place**.

11. Save the project.

Task 3 - Add walls, floors, roofs, and curtain systems.

1. Expand the 3D view by selecting it and typing **TW**.

2. Zoom in on one of the mass elements.

3. In the *Massing & Site* tab>Model by Face panel, click (Floor).

4. Select the floors and click (Create Floor).

5. Repeat the process with walls, roofs, and curtain systems.

6. Save and close the project.

Chapter Review Questions

1. Mass elements display by default in a view.

   a. True

   b. False

2. Which of the following elements was NOT created using the basic family types that come with the Autodesk Revit software?

   a.

   b.

   c.

   d.

3. What element(s) need to be placed first to create a blended sweep form?

   a. Two profiles on different work planes.

   b. A profile on an extrusion.

   c. More than two profiles on different levels.

   d. Two or more existing forms.

4. How do you cut a portion out of a conceptual mass element, as shown in Figure 1–100?

Figure 1–100

   a. Select the form and click 🖋 (Edit Profile).

   b. Create a void form in the mass element.

   c. Create another mass element and use ⬭ (Cut Geometry).

   d. Edit the form and add another profile to it.

5. Which of the mass form types is created from three or more profiles?

   a. Sweep

   b. Swept Blend

   c. Loft

   d. Extrusion

6. The start of a mass form is a sketch. How do you place a sketch on another form, as shown in Figure 1–101?

Figure 1–101

a. Select the **Draw** tool that you want to use, then use the **Draw on Face** tool.

b. Select the **Draw** tool that you want to use, then use the **Draw on Work Plane** tool.

c. Select the **Draw** tool that you want to use, then set the *Placement Plane* to a **Level**.

7. How do you move a sketch from one plane to another plane, as shown in Figure 1–102?

Figure 1–102

a. Change the *Placement Plane*.

b. Use the **Move** command.

c. Change the *Host*.

d. Use the **Align** command.

8. What must be in place before you can add a floor to a mass element, as shown in Figure 1–103?

Figure 1–103

a. Additional mass elements at each floor.

b. Sketches for each floor.

c. An additional floor parameter in Properties.

d. Mass floor elements at each floor.

Command Summary

Button	Command	Location
	Cut Geometry	• **Ribbon:** *Modify* tab>Geometry panel
	Edit In-Place	• **Ribbon:** *Modify	Mass* tab>Model panel
	Edit Work Plane	• **Ribbon:** *Modify	Mass* tab>Work Plane panel
	In-Place Mass	• **Ribbon:** *Massing & Site* tab> Conceptual Mass panel
	Load Family	• **Ribbon:** *Modify	Place Mass* tab> Mode panel
	Paint	• **Ribbon:** *Modify* tab>Geometry panel
	Place Mass	• **Ribbon:** *Massing & Site* tab> Conceptual Mass panel
	Place on Face	• **Ribbon:** *Modify	Place Mass* tab> Placement panel
	Place on Work Plane	• **Ribbon:** *Modify	Place Mass* tab> Placement panel
	Show Mass by Form and Floors	• **Ribbon:** *Massing & Site* tab> Conceptual Mass panel>expand Show Mass
	Show Mass by View Settings	• **Ribbon:** *Massing & Site* tab> Conceptual Mass panel>expand Show Mass
Conceptual Mass Environment		
	Add Edge	• **Ribbon:** *Modify	Form* tab>Form Element panel • **Right-click:** Add Edge
	Add Profile	• **Ribbon:** *Modify	Form* tab>Form Element panel • **Right-click:** Add Profile
	Create Form	• **Ribbon:** *Modify	Place Lines* tab> Form panel
	Divide Surface	• **Ribbon:** *Modify	Form* tab>Divide panel
	Draw on Face	• **Ribbon:** *Modify	Place Lines* tab> Draw panel
	Draw on Work Plane	• **Ribbon:** *Modify	Place Lines* tab> Draw panel
	Point Element	• **Ribbon:** *Modify	Place Lines* tab> Draw panel
	Model Line	• **Ribbon:** *Modify	Form* tab>Draw panel

	Reference Line	• **Ribbon:** *Modify	Form* tab>Draw panel
	Reference Plane	• **Ribbon:** *Modify	Form* tab>Draw panel
	X-Ray	• **Ribbon:** *Modify	Form* tab>Form Element panel • **Right-click:** X-Ray
	Void Form	• **Ribbon:** *Modify	Lines* tab>Form panel>expand Create Form

From Massing to Building

	Create Roof	• **Ribbon:** *Modify	Place Roof by Face* tab>Multiple Selection panel
	Curtain System (by Face)	• **Ribbon:** *Massing & Site* tab>Model by Face panel
	Floor (by Face)	• **Ribbon:** *Massing & Site* tab>Model by Face panel
	Mass Floors	• **Ribbon:** *Modify	Mass* tab>Model panel
	Related Hosts	• **Ribbon:** *Modify	Mass* tab>Model panel
	Roof (by Face)	• **Ribbon:** *Massing & Site* tab>Model by Face panel
	Wall (by Face)	• **Ribbon:** *Massing & Site* tab>Model by Face panel
	Update to Face	• **Ribbon:** *Modify	Multi-Select* tab>Model by Face panel

Space Planning and Area Analysis

Space planning using rooms and areas can be used in conceptual design and as part of the Building Information Model. The tools that come with Autodesk® Revit® are very powerful and enable you to lay out rooms in a building and track room information through all of the phases of a project. If you are working with rentable spaces, you can also add similar elements that keep track of the areas in a project. Both rooms and areas can have customized views that use color schemes that show the information graphically.

Learning Objectives in This Chapter

- Add rooms, room boundaries, and room tags to a project.
- Create area plans.
- Place area boundaries and areas.
- Set up a color scheme in a view.
- Define new color schemes by value and by range.

2.1 Space Planning

The room element is a powerful tool in the Autodesk® Revit® software. With this element, you can set up information to use in schedules and color diagrams to help present data or do take-offs. They also contain area, perimeter, and volume information about each room as well as the room name and number, as shown in Figure 2–1.

Figure 2–1

- Most walls, roofs, floors, ceilings, columns, and curtain systems are *Room Bounding* elements. One exception is the retaining wall type, which typically does not enclose rooms.

- You can add room separation lines to create rooms that are not bounded by walls.

- You can place room elements without any original bounding elements. They expand to fit any boundary that later encloses them.

How To: Create Rooms in a Plan

1. Draw the walls and other bounding elements that you want to have in your building.

2. In the *Architecture* tab>Room & Area panel, click ⊠ (Room) or enter **RM**.

3. In the *Modify | Place Room* tab>Tag panel, click ⌐① (Tag on Placement) if you want to include a tag as you place the room.

4. Use the Options Bar (shown in Figure 2–2) to:
   - Set the *Upper Limit* and *Offset*.
   - Set the *Orientation* of the tag and the *Leader*.
   - Select a *Room* name from the drop-down list (if room names have been previously created in a schedule).

Modify | Place Room   Upper Limit: Level 1 ▼ Offset: 4000.0   ▣ Horizontal ▼ ☐ Leader   Room: New   ▼

Figure 2–2

5. Move the cursor into a boundary area and click to place the room, as shown in Figure 2–3. Or, in the *Modify | Place Room* tab>Room panel, click ▨ (Place Rooms Automatically) to add rooms to every bounding area.

   - Select one room and set the first number before placing rooms automatically so they will increment as expected.

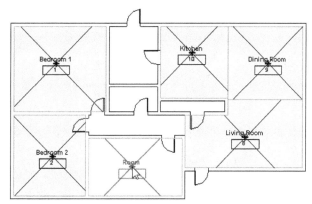

Figure 2–3

6. Continue adding rooms.

- In the *Modify | Place Room* tab>Room panel, click

  ☐ (Highlight Boundaries) to display all of the bounding objects in the project in orange. An alert box displays a warning that the room bounding elements are highlighted. When you close the alert box, it toggles off the highlighting of the bounding objects.

Hint: Setting Up Views to Show Rooms

Rooms do not display in views by default, so it can help to create views specifically for rooms. To do this, duplicate an existing plan or elevation view. Then, in the Visibility/Graphic Overrides dialog box, in the *Model Categories* tab, toggle on **Rooms**, then expand **Rooms** to toggle on **Interior Fill** and/or **Reference** to show the crossing lines.

Room Separation Boundaries

Boundaries for rooms can also be defined by room separation lines. Use these where you might not have a wall to separate the areas, but still want to specify them as different rooms. For example, in a house you can have a kitchen, dining area, and living area in a larger room that is not separated by walls, as shown in Figure 2–4.

Figure 2–4

How To: Create Room Separation Boundaries

1. In the *Architecture* tab>Room & Area panel, click ⬛ (Room Separator).
2. In the *Modify | Place Room Separation* tab>Draw panel, use the sketch tools to draw the edges of the boundary. Click

   ⬛ (Modify) to end the command.

3. Use ⬛ (Room) to add rooms in the areas bounded by the separation lines.

- You can edit room separation lines by splitting, trimming, etc.

Modifying Rooms

To select a room, hover the cursor over it until you see the reference lines (crossing lines) highlight, as shown in Figure 2–5. Then, select one of the reference lines to select the room.

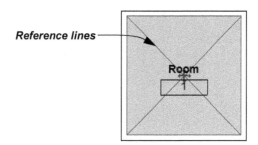

Figure 2–5

- When a room is selected, you can modify its Properties, as shown in Figure 2–6.

You can select several rooms at once to add the same information to all of them. <Ctrl> lets you add to your selection and <Shift> removes items from your selection group.

Figure 2–6

- You can also modify the vertical height of rooms in sections by using controls, as shown in Figure 2–7, or temporary dimensions.

Figure 2–7

Adding Room Tags

The Room Tag command is separate from other tag commands.

Room Tags can be added during or after rooms are added to a project. There are three room tag types: **Room Tag**, **Room Tag With Area**, and **Room Tag With Volume**, as shown in Figure 2–8.

Figure 2–8

How To: Place a Room Tag

1. Place rooms without tags in the project.
2. In the *Architecture* tab>Room & Area panel, click ⬚ (Tag Room) or in the *Annotate* tab>Tag panel, click ⬚ (Room Tag) or enter **RT**.
3. In Properties, select the tag type.
4. Click in the room you want to tag and repeat to tag as many rooms as needed.

- Rooms can be tagged in plan or section views.

- Rooms can be tagged using ⬚ (Tag All Not Tagged).

- To change the room name or number, select the tag and click on the name or number to modify it, as shown in Figure 2–9.

Figure 2–9

- If you delete a room tag, the room is not deleted.

- If you delete a room, the tag is deleted as well.

- If you select a tag, you can modify the *Orientation* and add or remove a *Leader* in Properties or the Options Bar, as shown in Figure 2–10.

Figure 2–10

- If you move a tag outside its room without a leader, it loses the association, as shown in Figure 2–11. You can add a leader or manually move it back in the room to re-associate it.

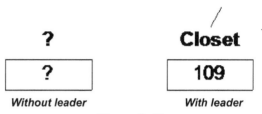

Without leader *With leader*

Figure 2–11

Room Schedules

Room schedules are used to keep track of data included in a room, such as the name, number, occupancy, area, and finishes. In the schedule you can select multiple rooms and apply the same information to them all.

- Room schedules can include standard building components, such as the room schedule shown in Figure 2–12.

	<Room Schedule>		
A	B	C	D
Number	Name	Department	Room Style
101	Office	Sales	Office-Standard
102	Office	Sales	Office-Standard
103	Workroom	Sales	Workroom
104	Office	Accounting	Office-Standard
105	Office	Accounting	Office-Standard
106	Office	Accounting	Office-Standard
107	Reception	Acounting	Reception
108	Office	Accounting	Office-Executive

Typical room schedule

Figure 2–12

Key schedules, such as the Finish Schedule shown in Figure 2–13, are also created from rooms.

<Finish Schedule>				
A	B	C	D	E
Key Name	Base Finish	Floor Finish	Wall Finish	Ceiling Finish
Corridor	Vinyl	Carpet	Painted	Ceiling Tile
Office-Executive	Wood	Wood	Painted	Ceiling Tile
Office-Standard	Vinyl	Carpet	Painted	Ceiling Tile
Reception	Vinyl	Carpet	Painted	Ceiling Tile
Workroom	Vinyl	Tile	Painted	Ceiling Tile

Typical finish schedule (key schedule)

Figure 2–13

Room Settings

You can set the way the Autodesk Revit software calculates volumes and boundary locations. In the *Architecture* tab>Room & Area panel, expand the panel title and click (Area and Volume Computations) to open the dialog box, as shown in Figure 2–14.

Figure 2–14

*   Calculating volumes slows down the speed of working in a project. You might only want to toggle it on before you do an evaluation.

Practice 2a | Space Planning

Practice Objectives

- Set up a view that displays rooms.
- Add rooms and room separation lines to a project.
- Review a room schedule.

In this practice, you will set up a view that displays rooms, add rooms, room separation lines, and room tags to an existing project. You will modify the room tags and give each room a name, as shown in Figure 2–15. Finally, you will review a room schedule and modify some of the contents.

Figure 2–15

Task 1 - Create a view and add rooms.

1. In the practice files folder, open **Medical-Office-Rooms-M.rvt**.

2. Duplicate the **Floor Plans: Level 1** view and rename it **Level 1 - Rooms**.

3. Open the Visibility/Graphic Overrides dialog box.

4. In the *Model Categories* tab, expand *Rooms* and select **Interior Fill**. Click **OK**.

5. In the *Architecture* tab>Room & Area panel, click ⊠ (Room) or enter **RM**. Verify that ⌐① (Tag on Placement) is on.

6. Place the first room in the upper left corner of the building and click ⌖ (Modify).

7. Zoom in on the room and select the tag, then select the number in the room tag. Change the tag's room number to **101**. You can press <Enter> or click anywhere outside of the room tag to finish. This causes the rest of the tags to automatically increment based on this number.

8. Start the **Room** command again.

   - To control the order of the room numbers, click in each room.
   - If the room number order does not matter, click ⊠ (Place Rooms Automatically).
   - Do not change the room names as you place them.

There is no way to mass change the order it places the tags in.

9. After you have placed all of the rooms, click ⌖ (Modify) to end the command. Zoom in and start naming them, as shown in Figure 2–16.

Figure 2–16

- To modify one room name at a time, click on the room tag and type a new name.
- To modify several rooms that need the same name, select the room elements (not the tags) and, in *Properties,* enter the name for the selected set of rooms.

10. Save the project.

Task 2 - Add room separation lines.

1. In the *Architecture* tab>Room & Area panel, click (Room Separator).

2. Draw a line across the opening at the elevator. The Entry room remains, but the elevator area does not have a room, as shown in Figure 2–17. Click (Modify) to end the command.

Figure 2–17

3. Add a room and name it **Elevator**.

If you have trouble selecting the tag, press <Tab> to cycle through the elements your cursor is hovering over.

The room number might be different in your drawing.

4. In the large room in the upper right corner, use room separation lines to divide the area, as shown in Figure 2–18. (Room sizes don't have to be exact.) Add rooms to the new spaces and modify the room tag names and numbers.

Figure 2–18

5. Save the project.

Task 3 - Review a room schedule.

---

1. In the Project Browser, expand the **Schedule/Quantities** node and select **Room Schedule**. The list of rooms displays, as shown in Figure 2–19.

   • Your room names might be associated with different numbers.

<Room Schedule>				
A	B	C	D	E
Number	Name	Area	Department	Occupancy
101	Entry	26 m²		
102	Stairs	13 m²		
103	Entry	36 m²		
104	Reception	31 m²		
105	Room	7 m²		
106	Office	45 m²		
107	Patient	11 m²		
108	Patient	11 m²		

Figure 2–19

2. Add information to the *Department* and *Occupancy* columns for individual rooms or groups of rooms. This can be done in plan view by selecting on the room(s) and adding the information in properties or within the schedule.

3. Save and close the project.

2.2 Area Analysis

Rooms calculate areas based on walls and other room bounding elements. However, you might need to define areas that extend across a variety of rooms. In addition, if you are working in a leasing situation, you might need to work with standard building rentable area definitions, as shown in Figure 2–20.

The Area Analysis tools in the Autodesk Revit software can accomplish these and related tasks. Many of the processes for area analysis are similar to those for rooms, such as defining boundaries, adding tags, and creating schedules.

Figure 2–20

Creating Area Plans

You must create an area plan before you can use the Area tools. The plan can provide the overall area of the building footprint, as shown in Figure 2–21, or it can be subdivided into additional areas.

Automatic boundary lines for Rentable space are on the inside of the exterior walls. For Gross Building area plans, the boundary lines are on the outside of the exterior walls.

Area plan with exterior boundaries

Figure 2–21

How To: Create an Area Plan

1. In the *Architecture* tab>Room & Area panel, expand ⊠ (Area) and click ⬚ (Area Plan).

2. In the New Area Plan dialog box, in the *Type* drop-down list, select the type of area plan that you want to create, as shown in Figure 2–22. The standard templates include two types: **Rentable** and **Gross Building**.

Figure 2–22

- If the **Do not duplicate existing views** option is selected, you will only see views that have not been used to create an area plan.

3. Select the level you want to create the area plan view. You can select more than one if needed.

4. Click **OK**.

5. An alert box opens, as shown in Figure 2–23. Click **Yes**.

If you do not automatically create boundary lines around the external walls, you need to add them later.

Figure 2–23

- Area plans are created for the selected levels. Each area plan is a separate view. They are listed in the Project Browser in the *Area Plans* area and divided by type, as shown in Figure 2–24.

Figure 2–24

Placing Area Boundaries

The area's type controls the precise location of boundary lines with respect to the walls. For a description of the area measurement rules for each area type, see the Autodesk Revit Help files.

The next step in creating an area analysis is to add *area boundary* lines in the area plan to define sections of the building, such as offices, stores, and common areas, as shown in Figure 2–25.

Area boundaries displayed in heavy lines

Figure 2–25

- Area boundaries display in a blue/purple line color.
- Gross Building area plans automatically include the area element.

How To: Create an Area Boundary

1. Open the Area Plan you want to work in.
2. In the *Architecture* tab>Room & Area panel, click ⬚ (Area Boundary).
3. In the Options Bar, select **Apply Area Rules** so that the boundary lines will move to the face or center of the walls according to the type of area you specify later.
4. In the *Modify | Place Area Boundary* tab>Draw panel, use the sketch tools to draw the boundaries or select walls to specify them. Use the modify tools, such as **Trim/Extend to Corner**, as needed.

Adding Areas

Once you have created the area plan and added boundaries to separate areas, you are ready to add area elements, as shown in Figure 2–26. These elements are similar to rooms in that they include much more than just a name for the area.

Figure 2–26

- To have the area background display, in the Visibility/Graphic Overrides dialog box, expand *Areas* and select **Color Fill**.

- Area information can be displayed in Gross Area or Rentable Area Schedules that include the area, name, type, and other options.

How To: Add Areas

1. In the *Architecture* tab>Room & Area panel, expand ⊠ (Area) and click ⊠ (Area).
2. Move the cursor over the closed area boundaries on the area plan to highlight the area. Click to place the area within the boundary. You can specify tags for the areas as you go.
3. Continue placing areas as needed.

- When you select one or more area elements, you can set the *Area Type* in Properties, as shown in Figure 2–27. Items that are grayed out (such as the *Area* and *Perimeter*) are automatically updated.

Figure 2–27

- Area types include **Building Common Area**, **Office Area**, **Exterior Area** (such as a patio or balcony), **Floor Area** (utility rooms and corridors), **Major Vertical Penetration**, and **Store Area** (retail), as shown above in Figure 2–27.

- Modifying the area boundaries or associated walls changes the calculated area in the tag.

- In the *Architecture* tab>Room & Area panel, click ⊠ (Tag Area) if you need to add area tags later.

- You can also use 🏳① (Tag All Not Tagged).

How To: Create Area Schemes

1. In the *Architecture* tab>Room & Area panel, expand the panel title and click (Area and Volume Computations).
2. In the dialog box, select the *Area Schemes* tab.
3. Click **New** to add a new scheme, as shown in Figure 2–28.

Area and Volume Computations

Computations   Area Schemes

	Name	Description		
1	Gross Building	Total Constructed Area of a Building		New
2	Rentable	Area Measurements Based on the Standard Method for Measuring Floor		Delete
3	Area Scheme 1	Area Measurements Based on the Standard Method for Measuring Floor		

Figure 2–28

4. Rename the scheme and add a description.

• New schemes use the same area types as the rentable scheme and include settings for area calculations and various area boundary locations. These are used in the color schemes.

• To create an area plan with the newly created area scheme, create a new area plan.

Practice 2b

Area Analysis

Practice Objectives

- Create a gross area plan and a rentable area plan.
- Modify area types in a schedule.
- Place plans and schedules on a sheet.

In this practice, you will use the Area Analysis tools to create a gross area plan and a rentable area plan. You will then add area boundary lines and areas, as shown in Figure 2–29, and modify the area types using an area schedule.

Figure 2–29

- The scale has been changed for clarity.

Task 1 - Create a gross area plan.

1. In the practice files folder, open **Medical-Office-Areas-M.rvt**. You should be on **Floor Plans: Level 1**.

2. In the *Architecture* tab>Room & Area panel, expand ⊠ (Area) and click ⬚ (Area Plan).

3. In the New Area Plan dialog box, set the *Type* to **Gross Building** and select **Level 1**. Click **OK**.

- If an alert box displays, click **Yes**. The gross area plan is created with boundary lines on the outside of the external walls, as shown in Figure 2–30.

Figure 2–30

4. In the *Architecture* tab>Room & Area panel, expand

   ⊠ (Area) and click ⊠ (Area). Click in the middle of the building to place the area as shown in Figure 2–31.

   - To see the area, open the Visibility/Graphic Overrides dialog box, expand *Areas*, and select **Interior Fill**.

Figure 2–31

5. Save the project.

Task 2 - Create a rentable area plan.

1. In the *Architecture* tab>Room & Area panel, expand (Area) and click (Area Plan).

2. In the New Area Plan dialog box, set the *Type* to **Rentable** and select **Level 1**. Click **OK**.

3. In the alert box, click **Yes** to create boundary lines at external walls. The area boundary is on the inside wall of the building, as shown in Figure 2–32. No areas are created automatically.

Figure 2–32

4. Open the Visibility/Graphic Overrides dialog box, expand *Areas*, and select **Interior Fill**. While you are still in the dialog box, toggle off **Rooms** completely to ensure that you do not select them by mistake.

5. In the *Architecture* tab>Room & Area panel, click ⊠ (Area Boundary). Use ⚲ (Pick Lines) and select the walls shown in Figure 2–33. Modify the lines as needed to create closed boundaries.

Figure 2–33

6. In the *Architecture* tab>Room & Area panel, expand ⊠ (Area) and click ⊠ (Area). Place areas and rename them, as shown in Figure 2–34.

Figure 2–34

7. Save the project.

Task 3 - Change area types using a schedule.

1. Open the **Schedules/Quantities: Area Schedule (Rentable)** view. The areas are listed but all of the *Area Types* are set to the default **Building Common Area**, as shown in Figure 2–35.

<Area Schedule (Rentable)>		
A	B	C
Name	Area Type	Area
Entrance	Building Common Area	27 m²
Tenant 1	Building Common Area	44 m²
Tenant 2	Building Common Area	81 m²
Tenant 3	Building Common Area	230 m²
Hall	Building Common Area	22 m²
Stair	Building Common Area	27 m²
Entrance	Building Common Area	29 m²

Figure 2–35

2. Change the area types in the schedule, as shown in Figure 2–36. The *Area* values change as the *Area Type* is modified.

<Area Schedule (Rentable)>		
A	B	C
Name	Area Type	Area
Entrance	Building Common Area	26 m²
Tenant 1	Office Area	44 m²
Tenant 2	Office Area	81 m²
Tenant 3	Office Area	229 m²
Hall	Building Common Area	22 m²
Stair	Major Vertical Penetration ▼	28 m²
Entrance	Building Common Area	29 m²
	Office Area	
	Exterior Area	
	Floor Area	
	Major Vertical Penetration	
	Store Area	

Figure 2–36

3. Save the project.

4. If you have time, create an additional Rentable area plan for Level 2.

5. Add area boundaries to define several areas on Level 2, and add areas to them.

Task 4 - Add the schedules to a sheet.

1. Create a new sheet file using the default title block.

2. Add the rentable area plan(s) and schedule to the sheet, as shown in Figure 2–37.

3. Select a view, from the Modify | Viewports>Viewport panel,

   select (Activate View) and do the following:

   • Toggle off the elevation markers in the area plans before you add them to the sheet so that they will fit.

   • Toggle off the area interior fill (this does not typically need to print).

Figure 2–37

4. Double click outside the view when finished to deactivate the view.

5. Save and close the Project.

2.3 Creating Color Schemes

Color Schemes added to views show information about rooms and areas. For example, if you add data to the room properties, such as Department or Occupancy, you can create a color scheme showing the groups using rooms. If you are using areas, you can identify the area types on an area plan, as shown in Figure 2–38.

Rentable Area Legend

Building Common Area

Major Vertical Penetration

Office Area

Figure 2–38

How To: Set Up a Color Scheme in a View

1. Create or duplicate a view for the color scheme.

2. In the *Annotate* tab>Color Fill panel, click ▤ (Color Fill Legend) and place the legend in the view.

3. In the dialog box, select the *Space Type* and *Color Scheme* (as shown in Figure 2–39) and click **OK.** The color scheme is applied to the view, as shown in Figure 2–40.

Figure 2–39   **Figure 2–40**

- You can also select a Color Scheme and place the legend later. In Properties, click the button next to the *Color Scheme*, as shown in Figure 2–41. Then, in the Edit Color Scheme dialog box, in the *Schemes* area, select the *Category* and an existing scheme.

Figure 2–41

- If you change the **Color Scheme** in the View Properties dialog box, it also updates the associated legend.

- You can edit the color scheme through properties or select the **Color Fill Legend** and, in the M*odify | Color Fill Legend* tab>Scheme panel, click (Edit Scheme).

You can set the Color Scheme Location in Properties.

• The color fill of the scheme can display in background or the foreground of the view, as shown in Figure 2–42. This impacts how components display as well as whether or not the color fill stops at the walls.

Color fill in background   **Color fill in foreground**

Figure 2–42

How To: Define a Color Scheme

1. In View Properties, click the button next to the *Color Scheme* parameter, or in the *Architecture* tab>Room & Area panel, expand the panel title and click ⬚ (Color Schemes).
2. In the Edit Color Scheme dialog box, *Schemes* area, select a *Category*: **Areas (Gross Building)**, **Areas (Rentable)**, or **Rooms**, as shown in Figure 2–43.

Figure 2–43

• Additional options for MEP related elements may also be available, including: Ducts, HVAC Zones, Pipes, and Spaces.

3. Select an existing scheme and click ⬚ (Duplicate).
4. In the New color scheme dialog box, enter a new name and click **OK**.
5. In the Edit Color Scheme dialog box, in the *Scheme Definition* area, enter a name for the *Title* of the color scheme. This displays when the legend is placed in the view.

6. In the Color drop-down list, select an option, as shown in Figure 2–44. The available parameters depend on the type of scheme you are creating.

Figure 2–44

7. Select the **By value** or **By range** option to set how the color scheme displays.

8. Click (Add Value) to add more rows to the scheme, as shown in Figure 2–45. Modify the visibility (*Visible* column), *Color*, and *Fill Pattern* as required.

Figure 2–45

9. In the *Options* area, select **Include elements from linked files** if you are using linked files.
10. Click **OK** to finish.

• Click (Move Rows Up) or (Move Rows Down) to change the order of rows in the list.

• To remove a row, select it and click (Remove Value). This option is only available if the parameter data is not being used in the room or area elements in the project.

Color Schemes By Value

If you select the **By value** option, you can modify the visibility, color, and fill pattern of the scheme. The value is assigned by the parameter data in the room or area object.

- Values are automatically updated when you add data to the parameters used in the color scheme. For example, if you create a color by room *Name* and then add another room name in the project, it is also added to the color scheme.

Color Schemes By Range

If you select the **By range** option, you can modify the *At Least* variable and the *Caption*, as well as the visibility, color, and fill pattern, as shown in Figure 2–46.

Figure 2–46

- Only the **Area** and **Perimeter** parameters can be set by range.

- Click **Edit Format...** to modify the units display format.

- When you add rows, the new row increments according to the previous distances set or double the value of the first row.

Practice 2c

Create Color Schemes

Practice Objectives

- Apply a color scheme to a view.
- Add a color scheme legend.
- Create **By value** and **By range** color schemes.

In this practice, you will add an existing color scheme and a legend to a view, as shown in Figure 2–47. You will also create and apply color schemes **By value** for room names and **By range** for rentable area sizes.

Rentable Area Legend

- Building Common Area
- Major Vertical Penetration
- Office Area

Figure 2–47

Task 1 - Apply a color scheme.

1. In the practice files folder, open **Medical-Office-Colors-M.rvt**.

2. Duplicate the **Area Plans (Rentable)**: **Level 1** view and name it **Level 1 - Rentable Area**.

3. In the *Annotate tab*>Color Fill panel, click ▤ (Color Fill Legend) and click to the left of the building to place the legend.

4. In the Choose Space Type and Color Scheme dialog boxes, set the *Space Type* to **Areas (Rentable)** and the *Color Scheme* to **Rentable Area**. Click **OK**.

5. The Legend and floor plan are set to the appropriate color fill, as shown in Figure 2–47.

6. Save the project.

Task 2 - Create a color scheme.

1. Duplicate with detailing the **Area Plans (Rentable)**: **Level 1 - Rentable Area** view and name it **Level 1 - Rentable Area by Size**.

2. Select the legend and in the *Modify | Color Fill Legends* tab> Scheme panel, click (Edit Scheme).

3. Click (Duplicate) to create a copy of the existing area color scheme and name it **Rentable Area by Size**.

4. In the *Scheme Definition* area, enter **Rentable Area by Size** for the *Title* and select **Area** in the Color drop-down list.

    *   Note that any time a warning about colors not being preserved displays, click **OK**.

5. Select **By range**. The default ranges display, as shown in Figure 2–48.

Scheme Definition

Title: Color: ○ By value

Rentable Area | Area   ▼ | ◉ By range   [Edit Format...]   1235 m² (Default)

At Least	Less Than	Caption	Visible	Color	Fill Pattern	Preview	In Use
	20.000 m²	Less than 20	☑	RGB 156-	Solid fill		No
20.000 m²		20 m² or mo	☑	PANTO	Solid fill		Yes

Figure 2–48

6. Set the **20.000 m²** *At Least* value to **60.000 m²**.

7. Click (Add Value). This should create a value of **120.000 m²**.

8. Select **120.000 m²** and click ✛ (Add Value) again. Continue working down the menu until you have **300.000 m²** in the *At Least* value list, as shown in Figure 2–49.

Figure 2–49

9. Click **OK** to close the dialog box. The new color scheme is applied to the view, as shown in Figure 2–50.

Figure 2–50

10. Save the project.

Task 3 - Create a room color scheme.

1. In the *Architecture* tab>Room & Area panel, expand the panel title and select 🖼 (Color Schemes).

2. In the Edit Color Scheme dialog box, set the *Category* to **Rooms**.

3. Click (Duplicate) to create a copy of the existing room color scheme. Name it **Room Names**.

4. In the *Scheme Definition* area, enter **Room Names** for the *Title* and select **Name** in the Color drop-down list.

5. The values are automatically applied according to the room names used in the project, as shown in part in Figure 2–51.

Figure 2–51

6. Click (Add Value) and create a new value named **Lab**. The new Lab value is set to **No** in the *In Use* column, as shown in Figure 2–52.

Figure 2–52

7. Modify the colors or fill patterns for the Lab. (Note that the default black is hard to see in the project.)

8. Click **OK**. The scheme is not applied to the current view when you create it this way.

9. Open the **Floor Plans: Level 1 - Rooms** view.

10. In Properties, select the **Color Scheme** button.

11. In the Edit Color Scheme dialog box, set the *Category* to **Rooms**, select the **Room Names** color scheme, and click **OK**.

12. In the *Annotate* tab>Color Fill panel, click (Color Fill Legend).

13. Place the legend to the side of the building. It automatically displays using the current color scheme, as shown in Figure 2–53.

Figure 2–53

14. Change the name of one of the offices to **Lab**. The color updates to match the Lab value you added to the color scheme.

15. Change the name of one of the exam rooms to **Mechanical**. A new value is automatically added to the color scheme, as shown in Figure 2–54.

Room Names

- Check-in
- Entry
- Equipment
- Exam
- Filling
- Hall
- Lab
- Mechanical
- Office
- Patient Records
- Physical Therapy
- Reception
- Recpetion
- Stairs
- Storage

Figure 2–54

16. Save and close the project.

Chapter Review Questions

1. Which of the following element types can define the boundaries of a room? (Select all that apply.)

   a. Walls

   b. Retaining Walls

   c. Floors

   d. Roofs

2. Where can you set the height of a room, as shown in Figure 2–55? (Select all that apply.)

Figure 2–55

   a. In Properties, before or after you place the room.

   b. In a section, after you place the room.

   c. In a 3D view.

   d. In the Options Bar, before you place the room.

3. In which type of view do you place areas?

   a. Floor Plans

   b. Sections

   c. Area Plans

   d. Elevations

4. Which of the following need to be in place before you add areas to an area plan, as shown in Figure 2–56?

Figure 2–56

a. Room Boundaries

b. Room Separation Lines

c. Area Separation Lines

d. Area Boundaries

5. If you want to have more than one color scheme that uses the same level and rooms, you need to create a view for each scheme.

a. True

b. False

6. If you are creating a color scheme to display the individual area of each room, as shown in Figure 2–57, which of the following do you use?

Figure 2–57

a. By value

b. By range

Command Summary

Button	Command	Location
	Activate View	• **Ribbon:** Modify|Viewports>Viewport panel
	Area	• **Ribbon:** *Architecture* tab>Room & Area panel, expand Area
	Area and Volume Computations	• **Ribbon:** *Architecture* tab>Room & Area panel, expand panel title
	Area Boundary	• **Ribbon:** *Architecture* tab>Room & Area panel
	Area Plan	• **Ribbon:** *Architecture* tab>Room & Area panel, expand Area
	Color Fill Legend	• **Ribbon:** *Annotate* tab>Color Fill panel
	Color Schemes	• **Ribbon:** *Architecture* tab>Room & Area panel, expand panel title
	Room	• **Ribbon:** *Architecture* tab>Room & Area panel • **Shortcut:** RM
	Room Separator	• **Ribbon:** *Architecture* tab>Room & Area panel
	Tag All Not Tagged	• **Ribbon:** *Architecture* tab>Room & Area panel, expand Tag Room or Tag Area
	Tag Area/ Area Tag	• **Ribbon:** *Architecture* tab>Room & Area panel or *Annotate* tab>Tags panel
	Tag Room/ Room Tag	• **Ribbon:** *Architecture* tab>Room & Area panel or *Annotate* tab>Tags panel • **Shortcut:** RT

Visualization

For the architectural community, one of the most powerful features of Autodesk® Revit® is the ability to create views that enable you to display the building design in its full 3D expression. Not only can you create perspective views, but you can also make any 2D or 3D view look realistic or like it was hand-sketched. You can create exploded orthographic views - each of which can help others understand your design. You can also visually test the design using sun studies that show exactly how sun and shadows would impact the building.

Learning Objectives in This Chapter

- Create perspective views using the Camera tool.
- Modify a view using graphic display options, such as Sketchy Lines and Depth Cueing.
- Displace elements in a view to create an exploded view.
- Set True North and the project location to prepare a project for solar studies.
- Graphically display sun locations and their impact on the project using the sun path with shadows.
- Create solar studies, including Still, Single Day, and Multi-Day studies.

3.1 Creating Perspective Views

Perspectives, as shown in Figure 3–1, provide more realistic views of buildings that can help designers visualize and pass on information to others who might not understand plans and elevations. They are easily created using the **Camera** command by specifying a camera location and a target.

Figure 3–1

- You can add, delete, modify, and move elements in 3D perspective views.

- Perspective views can be placed on sheets.

How To: Create a Perspective

1. Open a plan view.
2. In the Quick Access Toolbar (or the *View* tab>Create panel), expand 🏠 (3D View) and click 📷 (Camera).
3. In the Options Bar, select **Perspective** and set an *Offset* for the camera *From* one of the levels, as shown in Figure 3–2. This is the height of the camera.
    - To create orthographic views, clear the **Perspective** option and select a scale for the view.

Figure 3–2

4. Select a point on the drawing to place the camera.
5. Select another point for the target location, as shown in Figure 3–3.

To create an interior perspective, place the camera inside the room.

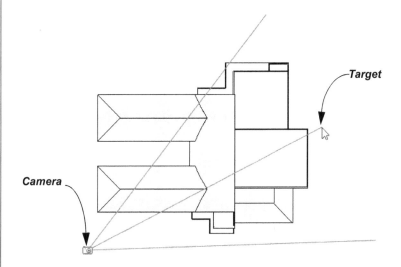

Figure 3–3

6. A new 3D view is created and opened, as shown in Figure 3–4.

Figure 3–4

7. In the Project Browser, right-click on the new 3D view and rename it.

• If you do not want the 3D View to be cropped, in the View Control Bar, click ⊞ (Do Not Crop View).

Modifying Perspectives

Perspectives can be modified by changing the camera information using controls or the camera properties. You can also modify the view size through a dialog box.

- Use the ViewCube or the mouse (<Shift>+ middle mouse button) to rotate the view.

- You can switch between Perspective and Isometric mode by right-clicking on the View Cube and selecting **Perspective** or **Orthographic**. You can also change this in the view properties.

- To change the field of view, select the shape handles of the crop region and manipulate them so that they show the required part of the building, as shown in Figure 3–5.

Figure 3–5

- To toggle off the box around the perspective, in Properties, clear the **Crop Region Visible** option or in the View Control Bar, click (Hide Crop Region).

- Change the *Visual Style* to **Shaded**, **Consistent Colors**, or **Realistic** to see a representation of the materials.

  - The (Realistic) visual style is ideal for managing light exposure, shadows, and Rich Photorealistic Content (RPC) components.

How To: Modify the Camera

1. Open the 3D camera view and one other view and tile them.
2. Select the edge of the camera view crop region and the camera displays in the other view.

- Another way to make a camera display in a plan view: right-click on the perspective view in the Project Browser and select **Show Camera**.

3. Drag the controls for the camera, target, and far clip plane, as shown in Figure 3–6, to new locations.

Target

Far clip plane

Camera

Figure 3–6

- The target is what the eye sees. The far clip plane needs to be located beyond the information you want to see in the view.

- You can make changes to cameras in Properties by scrolling down to the *Extents* and *Camera* sections, as shown in Figure 3–7.

Figure 3–7

- For a true 2-point perspective, ensure that both the *Target Elevation* and *Eye Elevation* are the same height.

How To: Modify View Size

1. In the *Modify | Cameras* tab>Crop panel, click (Size Crop).
2. In the Crop Region Size dialog box (shown in Figure 3–8), specify an exact *Width* and *Height* for the view.

Crop Region Size   ✕

Model Crop Size

Width: Height:

150 mm   113 mm

Change

◉ Field of view

○ Scale (locked proportions)

[OK]   [Cancel]   [Apply]   [Help]

Figure 3–8

- Select **Field of view** to resize both the *Height* and *Width* of the crop region.
- Select **Scale (locked proportions)** to lock the proportions of the crop region. When you change the width, the height adjusts proportionally.
- Alternatively, in the view you can use the control grips to resize the crop view, as shown in Figure 3–9.

Control Grips

Figure 3–9

Hint: Surface Transparency Sliders

While creating a perspective view, you are sometimes required to see behind a wall. You can toggle off an individual wall using **Hide in View>Elements**, or make the wall transparent as shown Figure 3–10.

Figure 3–10

How To: Adjust Transparency

1. Select the element(s), right-click, and select **Override Graphics in View>By Element...**
2. In the dialog box, expand the *Surface Transparency* area and adjust the slider bar as required, as shown in Figure 3–11.

Figure 3–11

- Surface patterns (such as brick) are not affected by the transparency setting; so, you may want to toggle them off in the *Surface Patterns* area, when working with transparency.

Practice 3a | Create Perspective Views

Practice Objective

• Create exterior and interior perspective views.

In this practice, you will create an interior perspective and an exterior perspective, as shown in Figure 3–12.

Figure 3–12

Task 1 - Create an exterior perspective view.

1. In the practice files folder, open **Midrise-Perspective-M.rvt**.

2. Open the **Floor Plans: Level 1** view.

3. In the *View* tab>Create panel, expand (3D View) and click (Camera).

4. Create an exterior perspective showing the front of the building (as shown above in Figure 3–12), name it **Front Perspective**, and set the *Visual Style* to **Consistant Colors**.

5. Modify the camera properties as needed to get a good view. Hold <Shift>+middle mouse button to rotate the view.

Task 2 - Create an interior perspective view.

1. Repeat the command and create an interior perspective as shown in Figure 3–13. Name it **Office Perspective**.

If the corner of the room does not display, change the far clip view.

Move the far clip view

Figure 3–13

2. Save the project.

3.2 Working with Graphic Display Options

Even without creating a rendering, you can set up striking views using graphic display options. These include tools for setting up the model display of surfaces and edges, shadows, sketchy lines for preliminary views, and added depth cueing for automatic lineweight control, and backgrounds as shown in Figure 3–14.

Figure 3–14

- In the View Control Bar, expand the **Visual Style** icon and select **Graphic Display Options...**, as shown in Figure 3–15. Additionally, you can enter **GD** to open the Graphic Display Options dialog box.

Figure 3–15

- The dialog box displays, as shown in Figure 3–16.

Graphic Display Options   ✕

▾ Model Display

           Style: Realistic   ⌄

                ☑ Show Edges

                ☑ Smooth lines with anti-aliasing

     Transparency: | 0

      Silhouettes: <none>   ⌄

▸ Shadows

▸ Sketchy Lines

▸ Depth Cueing

▸ Lighting

▸ Realistic

▸ Background

Save as View Template...

How do these settings affect view graphics?

OK   Cancel   Apply

Figure 3–16

- The settings that are selected in the Graphic Display Options dialog box can be saved as a View Template.

Model Display

In the Graphic Display Options dialog box, in the *Model Display* area, you can set the visual *Style* and *Transparency* (for all objects in the view) and select a linetype from the *Silhouettes* drop-down list. This override enables you to specify the type of lines used to outline various parts of a building in a view, as shown in Figure 3–17.

Default silhouette   *Silhouette override*

Figure 3–17

Hint: Adjusting Linework

To emphasize a particular line or change the look of a line in elevations and other views, modify the lines using the **Linework** command. If there is linework that you do not want to see, you can set the linework's line style to **<Invisible lines>**. These changes are view-specific, applying only to the view in which you make them, as shown in Figure 3–18.

Figure 3–18

- The **Linework** command can be used on project edges and cut edges of model elements, edges in imported CAD files, and edges in linked Autodesk Revit models.

How To: Adjust Linework

1. In the *Modify* tab>View panel, click (Linework) or enter the shortcut **LW**.
2. In the *Modify | Linework* tab>Line Style panel, select the line style you want to use from the list.
3. Move the cursor and highlight the line you want to change. Use <Tab> to toggle through the lines as required.
4. Click on the line to change it to the new line style.
5. Click on other lines as required, or return to the **Modify** command to finish.

If the line is too long or short, you can modify the length using the controls at the end of the line.

- The **Linework** tool overrides any other graphic changes to the view.

Shadows

In the Graphic Display Options dialog box, in the *Shadows* area, select **Cast Shadows**, as shown Figure 3–19. You can also select **Show Ambient Shadows**. Ambient shadows look more realistic as shadows are added to corners and other dark areas, but they make the view much darker.

Figure 3–19

Sketchy Lines

Autodesk Revit models can look polished even at the conceptual stage. Some people prefer to show clients a presentation that looks like it is hand-drawn. To do this, you can set up a view using sketchy lines, as shown in Figure 3–20.

Figure 3–20

- Sketchy lines can be used in all types of views, including: plans, elevations, sections, 3D orthographic, and perspective views.

- Datums (levels and grids) and annotation items are not impacted by sketchy lines.

- Views using sketchy lines can be exported to an image file, printed, and put on sheets.

How To: Modify a View Using Sketchy Lines

1. Set up a view where you want to apply a hand-drawn look.
2. In the View Control Bar, click on the **Visual Style** button and select **Graphic Display Options**. Alternatively, in Properties, beside the **Graphic Display Options...**, click **Edit...**.
3. In the Graphic Display Options dialog box, expand the *Sketchy Lines* area.
4. Select **Enable Sketchy Lines** and move the sliders for *Jitter* and *Extension*, as shown in Figure 3–21. Alternatively, you can type in a number in the box next to the slider bar.

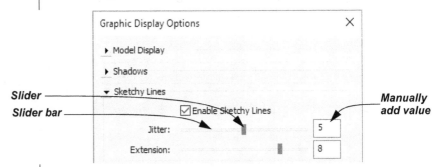

Figure 3–21

- *Jitter* controls how wavy the lines are and how many layers of lines there are. It varies from 0, where the lines are perfectly straight, to 10, which has multiple layers of wavy lines, as shown in Figure 3–22.
- *Extension* controls the length of the line beyond the end point. It varies from 0, where there is no extension, to 10 where the extension is longer, as shown in Figure 3–23.

Figure 3–22

Figure 3–23

5. Click **Apply** to see the change to the view.
6. When you are satisfied with the look, click **OK**.

Depth Cueing

Another important visual aid, called depth cueing, gives you a sense of depth by fading elements in the distance, as shown in Figure 3–24. This is set up in the Graphic Display Options dialog box.

Figure 3–24

- Depth cueing is specifically used for elevations and sections and does not work in plan or 3D views.

- The *Far Clipping* and *Far Clip Offset* parameters, which are set up in Properties (as shown in Figure 3–25), impact how depth cueing works. In the Far Clipping dialog box, select one of the clip methods, as shown in Figure 3–26, and click **OK**. Then, set a useful *Far Clip Offset* for the building.

Figure 3–25

Figure 3–26

- You can try changing the *Far Clip Offset* before adjusting the view in the Graphic Display Options dialog box, as depth cueing is based on the location of the front and back view clip planes.

How To: Establish a Sense of Depth in a View

1. Set up a view where you want to apply depth cueing
2. In Properties, set up a *Far Clipping* method and a *Far Clip Offset*.
3. Open the Graphic Display Options dialog box and expand *Depth Cueing*.
4. Select **Show Depth** and click **Apply** to see how the default settings work.
5. Move the sliders for *Fade Start/End Location* and *Fade Limit (%)* as required, as shown in Figure 3–27.

Figure 3–27

- *Fade Start/End Location* controls the start and end of the fading. *Near* and *Far* are the percentage away from the front and back view clip planes.

- The *Fade Limit (%)* intensity can be set from *Light* to *Dark*.

6. Click **Apply** to see the change to the view.
7. When you are satisfied with the look, click **OK**.

Background

In the *Background* area, in the Background drop-down list, select one of the following four options: **None**, **Gradient** or **Sky** (which give a default sky appearance and enable you to specify a ground color, as shown in Figure 3–28 and Figure 3–29), or **Image** (which enables you to select a custom background image).

Figure 3–28   **Figure 3–29**

Lighting and Photographic Exposure

When you are in the **Realistic** visual style, in the *Lighting* area (shown in Figure 3–30), you can set the *Sun Settings* and specify the intensity of the *Sun*, *Ambient Light*, and *Shadows*. You can also specify *Artificial Lights* if you have lighting fixtures in the project and want to specify which ones will be used in the view.

The concepts in the Lighting and Photographic Exposure areas are covered in more depth in Sun Studies and Rendering.

Figure 3–30

In the *Photographic Exposure* area (shown in Figure 3–31), you can modify the artificial lights to set the best exposure to a scene.

Figure 3–31

Practice 3b

Work with Graphic Display Options

Practice Objectives

- Use Sketchy Lines and other graphic display options.
- Set up a 3D view oriented to a 2D view.
- Investigate Depth Cueing.

In this practice, you will set up an elevation view of the front entrance and modify the look using Sketchy Lines. You will then duplicate the view and set it up to look more realistic, as shown in Figure 3–32. You will also create a 3D elevation view and modify another view using Depth Cueing and how the Far Clip plane and offset impacts the view.

Figure 3–32

Task 1 - Set up a view using Sketchy Lines.

1. In the practice files folder, open **Midrise-Display-M.rvt**.

2. In the Project Browser, duplicate the **Elevations (Building Elevation): South** view and rename it to **South Entry Prelim**.

3. Hide the level lines. (Select a level and enter **VH** to hide the category.)

4. In the View Control Bar, click ⌐⊞⊙ (Show Crop Region).

5. Modify the crop region so you are only seeing the entry area of the building, as shown in Figure 3–33.

Figure 3–33

6. In the View Control Bar, click ⌐⊞⊙ (Hide Crop Region). Type ZA to zoom to fit.

7. In Properties, beside Graphic Display Options, click **Edit...**.

8. In the Graphic Display Options dialog box, expand the *Sketchy Lines* area and select **Enable Sketchy Lines.**

9. Move the dialog box over to the side so you can see the view as you make changes, and click **Apply**.

10. Slide the *Jitter* bar to around **5** and click **Apply**. (You can also type 5 in the box next to the slider bar.) The lines take on a sketch-like look, as shown in Figure 3–34.

Figure 3–34

11. Try several different looks by manipulating the *Jitter* and *Extension* slider bars. Click **Apply** after each change to see the variations.

12. Click **OK** when you have the desired look.

13. Save the project.

Task 2 - Set up a view using shadows and the Realistic visual style.

---

1. Duplicate the **South Entry Prelim** view and name it **South Entry DD**.

2. Open the Graphic Display Options dialog box. (**Hint:** Enter **GD**).

3. In the Graphic Display Options dialog box, toggle off **Sketchy Lines** and click **OK**.

4. In the View Control Bar, click (Shadows Off) to toggle (Shadows On).

5. Try out the various visual styles to see how they look with the view. End on the **Realistic** visual style.

6. Open the Graphic Display Options dialog box.

7. In the *Model Display* area, deselect **Show Edges** and click **Apply** to see the changes. End with **Show Edges** selected.

8. Expand *Shadows*, select **Show Ambient Shadows**, and click **Apply** to see the changes.

9. Expand *Background* and test out several different options. Click **OK** and the background is applied, such as the gradient shown in Figure 3–35.

There are several image files you can use in the practice files Images folder.

Figure 3–35

10. Close all other views except the **South Entry Prelim** and **South Entry DD** views.

11. Enter **WT** to tile them and then **ZA** to zoom so they fit in each window. Enter **TW** to go back to viewing one view.

12. Save the project.

Task 3 - Create a 3D elevation view

1. Open the default 3D view.

2. Rename it **South Entry**.

3. Right-click on the ViewCube and select **Orient to View> Elevations>Elevation: South Entry DD**, as shown in Figure 3–36.

4. Test out several different visual styles and graphic display options with this view, as shown in Figure 3–37.

Figure 3–36

Figure 3–37

• While in the Realistic visual style, you cannot enable Depth Cueing but all other graphic display options are available.

5. Close the dialog box.

6. Save the project.

Task 4 - Apply Depth Cueing to a view.

1. Open the **Elevations: South** view.

2. Set the *Visual Style* to **Shaded**.

You may need to open Floor Plans Level 1 and adjust the Elevation Markers clipping.

3. Open the Graphic Display Options dialog box and toggle on **Show Depth**, but do not make any changes yet. Click **OK**.

4. In Properties, set *Far Clipping* to **Clip with line**. By default, the *Far Clip Offset* is set to **3048.0mm**. This distance is not deep enough to show the building so only the toposurface displays as shown in Figure 3–38.

Figure 3–38

5. Test several *Far Clip Offset* distances in increments of 3048 (e.g., 6096mm, 9144mm, 12192mm) and finish with **30000mm**. The building displays with a shaded roof.

6. Open the Graphic Display Options dialog box and make changes to the *Depth Cueing* options to fade the roof, as shown in Figure 3–39.

Figure 3–39

7. Save the project.

3.3 Adding Exploded Views

You can use displacement sets to create exploded views that can be used to explain a project or detail a complex detail. These views update as you work on a project, any other view does. They can be created in 3D perspective or orthographic views, such as that shown in Figure 3–40.

Figure 3–40

- Displaced views are full 3D views and can be rotated using the mouse or ViewCube.

How To: Displace Elements

1. Select the element or elements that you want to displace.
2. In the *Modify | <element type>* tab>View panel, click

    (Displace Elements).
3. In Properties, set the *X*, *Y*, and/or *Z Displacement* or use the drag controls on the face of the element, as shown in Figure 3–41.

Figure 3–41

4. To display projection lines from the original location to the displacement, in the *Modify | Displacement Set* tab>

   Displacement Set panel, click ✐ (Path).
5. Select the corner of the displaced element where you want to locate the path.

- When displacing a wall, elements (such as doors and windows) are also displaced. You can displace them separately by using <Tab> to select them once you have displaced the wall.

- Storefront curtain wall elements are not displaced with the walls in which they are located. You can add them to the displacement set or displace them separately.

- If you want to displace a door or window separately from a wall, press <Tab> until the element is highlighted and then follow the steps for displacing elements.

- If you no longer want an element to be displaced, select it, and in the *Modify | Displacement Set* tab>Displacement Set

   panel, click ⬚ (Reset).

- In a view that displays the displacements sets, in the View Control Bar, click (Highlight Displacement Sets). The displacement sets display in color with a rim around the edge of the view, as shown in Figure 3–42.

Figure 3–42

How To: Edit Displaced Elements

1. Select a displaced element.
2. In the *Modify | Displacement Set* tab>Displacement Set panel, click (Edit). The existing displacement set is highlighted.

3. Verify that (Add) is selected in the floating Edit Displacement Set panel and select the elements you want to include in the displacement set, as shown in Figure 3–43.

Figure 3–43

4. As you select the elements, they are moved into place and highlighted.

5. If you do not want an element to be in the displacement set, click ⌸ (Remove) and select the element. The element returns to place.

6. Click ✓ (Finish).

- It is sometimes easier to displace one element (such as a wall) and then add other elements to the set.

Practice 3c

Create an Exploded View

Practice Objectives

- Displace elements in a view to create an exploded view.
- Add elements to a displacement set.

In this practice, you will create a 3D view in which you will set up several displacement sets to create an exploded view of the building. You will also add an element to a set and place paths that display the location. An example of a finished view is shown in Figure 3–44 with the displacement sets highlighted.

Figure 3–44

Task 1 - Create displacement sets.

1. In the practice files folder, open **Midrise-Exploded-M.rvt**.

2. Open the **3D Views: 3D - Exploded** view.

3. Rotate the view so it is similar in orientation to that shown above in Figure 3–44.

4. Select the brick wall on the front left.

5. In the *Modify | Walls* tab>View panel, click 📷 (Displace Elements).

In this case, you need to move the control in the direction opposite to the arrow.

6. Use the control to drag it away from the building, as shown in Figure 3–45.

Figure 3–45

7. Select the hipped roof, click 🖾 (Displace Elements), and move it up using the control or Properties.

8. Select the first wall that you displaced. In the *Modify | Displacement Set* tab>Displacement Set panel, click

   🖾 (Edit).

9. In the Edit Displacement Set floating panel, ensure that

   🖾 (Add) is selected and click on the longer front brick wall. It moves to match the location, as shown in Figure 3–46.

Figure 3–46

10. Click 🖾 (Finish).

11. With the elements still selected, click 🖾 (Path).

12. Select the corners of each wall and the corners of the roof to place the lines.

13. Displace other elements of the building, as required.

14. Save the project.

3.4 Setting Up Solar Studies

The next step in enhancing your views is to get the sun in the correct place so that you can see how shadows impact your project. First, you need to establish the geographical location of the project and the true north direction. Then, you can graphically set year and time of day using the sun path, as shown in Figure 3–47. From there, you can create still, single day, and multi-day solar studies that show more accurate time settings.

Figure 3–47

In the View Control Bar, toggle on **Sun Path** and **Shadows**, as shown in Figure 3–48.

Toggle shadows off when you do not need them to conserve memory resources.

Figure 3–48

* The sun path and shadows can be used in 2D and 3D views.

Preparing for Solar Studies

The geographic location of a project and the true north orientation of the model on the site impact solar studies. Most buildings are modeled with north at the top of the primary axis, as shown in Figure 3–49. True north can be set in a site plan view, as shown in Figure 3–50.

Figure 3–49

Figure 3–50

- If you are working with a linked DWG file, you can use the geographic data stored in that file.

How To: Set True North

1. Duplicate the **Floor Plans: Site** view and rename it **Site - True North**.
2. In Properties, set the *Orientation* to **True North**, as shown in Figure 3–51.

Figure 3–51

3. In the *Manage* tab>Project Location panel, expand (Position) and click (Rotate True North).

---

4. In the Options Bar, enter a value for *Angle from Project to True North*, or select two points on the screen to define the angle (similar to the **Rotate** command). The entire project rotates, as shown in Figure 3–52.

Figure 3–52

How To: Manage the Location for a Project

1. In the *Manage* tab>Project Location panel, click

   (Location).

2. In the Location Weather and Site dialog box>*Location* tab, you can set the *Define Location by*: the **Default City List** (typically used for HVAC sizing), as shown in Figure 3–53, or **Internet Mapping Service** (typically used for energy analysis), as shown in Figure 3–54.

Figure 3–53

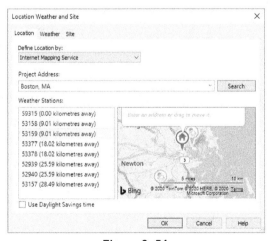

Figure 3–54

Using the Sun Path

If you want to graphically set the sun locations, you can use the sun path to specify the date and time of day by dragging the sun icon around the path or analemma, as shown in Figure 3–55.

Figure 3–55

How To: Use the Sun Path

1. In the View Control Bar, expand ⬚ (Sun Path Off) and click ⬚ (Sun Path On).
   - If you have not already applied the appropriate sun settings, an alert box displays. Select **Use the specified project location, date, and time instead** to apply the default settings. The other option will not display the sun.
2. Move the sun along the path to change the time of day.
3. Move the sun along the analemma to retain the time of day but change the month.

4. Click on the time of day or the month and change the number, as shown in Figure 3–56.

Figure 3–56

Creating Solar Studies

To create solar studies you will use the Sun Settings dialog box, where you can set up the information for still, single day, and multi-day options. Additionally, you can use several preset studies.

- Shadows need to be on to display the solar studies.

How To: Create Solar Studies

At least one solar study is always available.

1. In the View Control Bar, expand the Sun Path drop-down list and click **Sun Settings** or type **SU**, as shown in Figure 3–57. You can also access the Sun Settings in Properties, through the Graphic Display Options dialog box.

Figure 3–57

2. In the Sun Settings dialog box, *Solar Study* area, select the type of study you want to create: **Still**, **Single Day**, or **Multi-Day**.
3. In the *Presets* area, select an existing study and click (Duplicate).
4. In the Name dialog box, enter a name for the study and click **OK**.

- For **Still** studies, in the *Settings* area, specify the *Location*, *Date*, and *Time*, as shown in Figure 3–58.

Figure 3–58

*The **Sunrise to sunset** option automatically calculate the times based on the date.*

- For **Single Day** studies, in the *Settings* area (shown in Figure 3–59), specify the *Location*, *Date*, and *Time* (start and end). Select the *Time Interval* (**15**, **30**, **45 minutes** or **One hour**). The *Frames* value is read-only.

Figure 3–59

• For **Multi-Day** studies, in the *Settings* area, specify the *Date* range, and the *Time* and the *Time Interval*, which is typically set to **One day** or more, as shown in Figure 3–60.

Figure 3–60

5. Click **OK** to close the dialog box and apply the still solar study to the view.

Hint: Setting the Ground Plane

In each type of solar study, you can set the **Ground Plane at Level**, as shown on the left in Figure 3–61, or leave this option cleared. If you do not have site information in the drawing or you are working with an interior view, specify a level. If you have site information (topography) in the drawing, do not specify a level for the ground plane so that the shadows flow over the contours, as shown on the right in Figure 3–61.

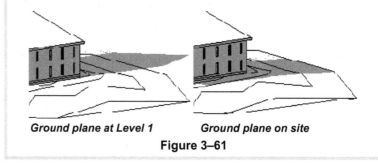

Ground plane at Level 1   *Ground plane on site*

Figure 3–61

How To: View Solar Studies

1. Toggle on shadows and ensure that you are in either a **Single Day** or **Multi-Day** solar study type.

2. In the View Control Bar, click ⚝ (Sun Path Off) and select **Preview Solar Study**, as shown in Figure 3–62.

Figure 3–62

3. In the Options Bar (shown in Figure 3–63), specify the frame at which you want to start and click ▶ (Play).

Figure 3–63

How To: Export Solar Studies

1. Toggle on shadows and ensure that you are in either a **Single Day** or **Multi-Day** solar study type.

2. In the *File* tab, expand ⬈ (Export)> 🎞 (Images and Animations), and then click 🖼 (Solar Study).

3. In the Length/Format dialog box, specify the *Output Length* and *Format*, as shown in Figure 3–64.

Figure 3–64

4. Click **OK**.

5. In the Export Animated Solar Study dialog box, navigate to a folder and specify a file name.

   • By default, the file name is the name of the project plus the name of the Solar Study.

6. Specify the file format, as shown in Figure 3–65, and click **Save**.

Figure 3–65

7. In the Video Compression dialog box, select the type of *Compressor*, as shown in Figure 3–66, and specify any other options. Click **OK**.

Figure 3–66

   • The new animation is processed and can be viewed using the related video software.

Practice 3d

Set Up Solar Studies

Practice Objectives

- Set the True North and establish the project location to prepare a project for solar studies.
- Create a Still solar study, a Single Day solar study, and a Multi-Day solar study.

In this practice, you will create solar studies for your location using the three methods: **Still** (as shown in Figure 3–67), **Single Day**, and **Multi-Day**.

Figure 3–67

Task 1 - Prepare the project for solar studies.

1. In the practice files folder, open **Midrise-Solar-M.rvt**.

2. Duplicate a copy of the **Floor Plans: Site** view and rename it **Site-True North**. Open the new view.

3. In Properties, set the *Orientation* to **True North**.

4. In the *Manage* tab>Project Location panel, expand 🏠 (Position) and click ↻ (Rotate True North).

5. In the Options Bar, set the *Angle from Project to True North* to **23°** from **East** and press <Enter> for it to take effect. The site plan rotates, as shown in Figure 3–68.

Figure 3–68

6. In the *Manage* tab>Project Location panel, click

   (Location).

7. In the *Location* tab, select your city, or one close to you, in the **Default City List** or from the **Internet Mapping Service** map. Select **Use Daylight Savings Time**, if this applies. Click **OK**.

Task 2 - Create a Still solar study.

---

1. Create a new default 3D view that shows the front of the building and the site. Rename the view to **Still Solar Study**.

You can also set up these options in the Graphic Display Options dialog box.

2. In the View Control Bar, set the *Visual Style* to

   (Consistant Colors) and enable (Shadows On).

3. In the View Control Bar, enable (Sun Path On). When the Sun Path - Sun Not Displayed dialog box opens, select **Use the specified project location, date and time instead**.

4. Expand (Sun Path On) and select **Sun Settings...**or type SU.

5. In the Sun Settings dialog box, S*olar Study* area, select **Still**.

6. In the *Settings* area, specify today's date and time. To easily get to today's date, expand and click **Today**, as shown in Figure 3–69.

Figure 3–69

7. Click **OK** to close the dialog box. The solar study displays according to your location and time, similar to that shown in Figure 3–70.

Figure 3–70

8. Type SU to select another day and time in the Sun Settings dialog box, and click **Apply** to see the results.

9. Save the project.

Task 3 - Create a Single Day solar study.

1. Duplicate the **Still Solar Study** view.

2. Rename the new view to **Single Day Solar Study**.

3. Toggle off the sun path.

4. Open the Sun Settings dialog box and create a new Single Day solar study - for today's date, from sunrise to sunset, with a *Time Interval* of **15 minutes**.

5. Click **OK** to close the dialog box.

6. In the View Control Bar, click (Sun Path Off) and select **Preview Solar Study**. (If this is not available, verify that the shadows are on.)

7. In the Options Bar, click (Play). The shadows move across the building, as shown for one frame in Figure 3–71.

Figure 3–71

Task 4 - Create a Multi-Day solar study.

1. Duplicate the **Single Day Solar Study** view.

2. Rename the new view as **Multi-Day Solar Study**.

3. Open the Sun Settings dialog box and create a new Multi-Day solar study, for one year at noon with a *Time Interval* of **One month**.

4. Click **OK** and preview the solar study animation.

5. Use ▷ (Next Frame) and step through each month.

6. Save the drawing.

Chapter Review Questions

1. How do you create a perspective view, as shown in Figure 3–72?

Figure 3–72

   a. Create a Default 3D view and, in Properties, modify the Camera settings.

   b. Create a Camera view.

   c. Create a Default 3D view and, in Properties, select **Perspective**.

   d. Create a Camera view and, in Properties, select **Perspective**.

2. Where can you set the Eye and Target Elevations of a camera?

   a. In Properties.

   b. In the Options Bar.

   c. In the View Control Bar.

   d. In the *Modify | Camera* tab in the ribbon.

3. Which of the following types of views can you customize to resemble a hand-drawn sketch? (Select all that apply.)

   a. Floor Plans

   b. Perspectives

   c. 3D Orthographic Views

   d. Elevations

4. When creating an exploded view, how do you add the dashed lines that connect to the origins, as shown in Figure 3–73?

Figure 3–73

a. Draw them using ⌐ (Detail Line).

b. Draw them using ⌐ (Model Line).

c. Select the displaced element, click ⬚ (Edit), and draw them.

d. Select the displaced element, click ✎ (Path), and select the corners of the displaced element.

5. How do you change the time of day when working with the sun path shown in Figure 3–74? (Select all that apply.)

Figure 3–74

a. Modify the sun path Properties.

b. Drag the sun along the path.

c. Change the time in the Options Bar.

d. Click on the time control.

6. To get the most accurate view of how the sun impacts your project, which of the following must be set before a solar study is produced?

a. The geographic location of the project site and the project's orientation to True North.

b. Nothing needs to be set.

c. The rotation of the building to Project North.

7. When creating a Multi-Day sun study, the *Time Interval* can be set to every 15 minutes.

a. True

b. False

Command Summary

Button	Command	Location
	Camera	• **Ribbon:** *View* tab>Create panel, expand 3D View • **Quick Access Toolbar:** expand 3D View
N/A	**Graphic Display Options**	• **Properties** • **View Control Bar: Expand Visual Styles** • **Shortcut:** GD
	Location	• **Ribbon:** *Manage* tab>Project Location panel
N/A	**Preview Solar Study**	• **View Control Bar:** Expand Sun Path
	Rotate True North	• **Ribbon:** *Manage* tab>Project Location panel, expand Position
	Shadows On	• **View Control Bar**
	Shadows Off	• **View Control Bar**
	Sun Path On	• **View Control Bar**
	Sun Path Off	• **View Control Bar**
N/A	**Sun Settings**	• **View Control Bar:** Expand Sun Path
Exploded Views		
	Displace Elements	• **Ribbon:** *Modify <elements type>* tab> View panel>Displace Elements
	Edit	• **Ribbon:** *Modify	Displacement Set* tab> Displacement Set panel>Edit
	Highlight Displacement Sets	• **View Control Bar**
	Path	• **Ribbon:** *Modify	Displacement Set* tab> Displacement Set panel>Path
	Reset	• **Ribbon:** *Modify	Displacement Set* tab> Displacement Set panel>Reset

Rendering

The most powerful way to show off a design is to create a rendering. Renderings provide a "real world" view that typical floor plans and elevations cannot match. Using a rendering, you can show materials, lighting, daylight, people, furniture, and plants as part of your design. You can use graduating levels of quality in your rendering as you prepare the view for a final, photorealistic rendering.

Learning Objectives in This Chapter

- Create a rendering of a view or a portion of a view.
- Set the rendering options.
- Add light fixtures and view light sources.
- Set up groups of lights so that you can control the lights that display in a rendering.
- Add people, plants, and other components to enhance your renderings.

4.1 Producing Basic Renderings

Rendering is a powerful tool where you display a photorealistic view of the model you are working on, such as the example shown in Figure 4–1. This can be used to help clients and designers alike to understand the building design in better detail. Renderings can be used as presentations for everything from code compliance to color schemes.

Figure 4–1

- While you can produce fairly elaborate renderings directly in the Autodesk® Revit® software, more extensive renderings are typically created in other software such as Autodesk® 3ds Max®.

- If you have an Autodesk Subscription, you can also render in the cloud using Autodesk A360 Rendering. The service will notify you when the rendering is complete. You can view, download, and modify completed renderings in the Render Gallery.

- All rendering done in Autodesk Revit is created using Autodesk Raytracer. This rendering engine accurately represents real-world materials by calculating light and its impact on materials as accurately as possible.

- If you are upgrading a model from previous versions, any Mental Ray settings are automatically mapped to the appropriate Raytracer settings. These settings are not maintained when upgrading.

Prepare Views for Rendering

To prepare a view for rendering, you need to:

- Create the 3D view.

- Verify that the materials you want are applied to the model elements.

- Toggle on shadows.

- Add lights and/or specify sun settings.

- Apply a background.

- Add Rich Photorealistic Content (RPC) components (such as plants, people, and cars).

Hint: Rendering 2D Views

Although only 3D views can be rendered, you can create a 3D view that looks like a 2D view. In a 3D view, right-click on the ViewCube and select **Orient to View** or **Orient to a Direction**. Set the view up using shadows and materials and render it, as shown in Figure 4–2.

Figure 4–2

- Materials and lighting are built into many of the elements in the Autodesk Revit model, including walls, windows, and light fixtures.

- The ⬜ (Realistic) visual style gives you a sense of what the rendered view might actually look like. It includes any RPC you might have added.

How To: Render a View - Basic Steps

This option only displays if you are in a 3D view.

1. In the View Control Bar, click (Show Rendering Dialog), enter **RR**, or in the *View* tab>Presentation panel, click

   (Render).

2. In the Rendering dialog box shown in Figure 4–3, set up the Rendering Settings for: *Quality*, *Output Settings*, *Lighting*, and *Background*.

Figure 4–3

3. Click **Render**.

4. The Rendering Progress dialog box opens, as shown in Figure 4–4. It closes when the rendering is complete if that option is selected.

Figure 4–4

5. In the *Image* area of the Rendering dialog box, click **Adjust Exposure...** to modify the brightness and other options.

Saving a rendering to a project significantly increases the file size.

6. Click **Save to Project...** to keep a copy of the rendering. Enter a name in the Save To Project dialog box (as shown in Figure 4–5) and click **OK**.

Figure 4–5

*The **Save to Project** and **Export** options are not available until a view is rendered.*

• Rendered views saved to the Project Browser can be printed and placed on sheets.

7. Click **Export...** to export a rendering as BMP, JPG, JPEG, PNG, or TIFF files.

• The new file can be brought back into the project using the **Image** command.

8. When you are finished with an on-screen rendering, click **Show the model** in the *Display* area to remove the rendering from the view.

- Rendering information is saved with the 3D view used to create the rendering. In Properties, in the *Camera* area beside *Rendering Settings*, click **Edit...** to bring up the Rendering Settings dialog box, as shown in Figure 4–6. You can modify the *Quality*, *Lighting*, *Background*, and adjust the exposure of the *Image*.

Figure 4–6

- Rendering settings can be included in a View Template and applied to other views.

Hint: Best Practices: Rendering a Region

The amount of time required to render an image is directly related to the complexity of the model and of the materials, the number of artificial lights, and the size or resolution of the image. To save time when you are developing the image, in the Render dialog box, select **Region** and place a region around some of the elements, as shown in Figure 4–7. It's also beneficial to go into Visibility/Graphic Overrides and turn off elements that are not seen in your rendering.

Figure 4–7

- Drag the box to move the entire region or drag the controls to resize the region.

- If some elements do not render as expected, check the materials. The material might be set to **<By Category>** rather than using a specific material.

Rendering Settings

Quality

The first setting you need to specify for a rendering is the *Quality*. You can select from a preset list (as shown in Figure 4–8) or create your own Custom (view specific) settings.

Figure 4–8

- Start with a draft quality image to verify that the materials and lights appear as you expect. Then, modify these elements and other settings and move to a higher quality output as you create a more realistic image. Only use high quality settings when you know you have the image you want.

Output Settings

Renderings can be set to the screen or to a printer. If you select the **Printer** option, you can select from a list of DPI (dots per inch) options. The *Width* and *Height* of the view are displayed in pixels and the image size is displayed in megabytes (MB), as shown in Figure 4–9.

Figure 4–9

Lighting

In the *Lighting* area in the Rendering dialog box, you can select a *Scheme* that defines the use of the sun and artificial light, set up the *Sun* settings, and work with the artificial lights in the model, as shown in Figure 4–10.

Figure 4–10

- Select from a variety of lighting schemes including **Exterior: Sun only, Exterior: Sun and Artificial, Exterior: Artificial only, Interior: Sun only, Interior: Sun and Artificial, Interior: Artificial only.**

- For the *Sun Setting*, click ⌐...⌐ (Browse) to access the dialog box to select, make, or edit other solar studies.

*The Artificial Lights
button is grayed out if
you are set to one of the
Sun Only lighting
schemes.*

- Click **Artificial Lights...** to set up the lights and light groups used in the rendering.

Background

In the *Background* area in the Rendering dialog box, you can set the *Style* for the sky. Select from several levels of cloud cover, a color, or an image, and specify the *Haze* level for any amount of clouds, as shown in Figure 4–11.

Figure 4–11

- The amount of clouds in a background impacts the overall quality of light in the rendering.

- When you select **Image**, you can specify any image file as the background.

- The **Transparent** option enables you to create a PNG or TIFF file that leaves the background transparent.

Image

Click **Adjust Exposure...** to open the Exposure Control dialog box, as shown in Figure 4–12. You can make the rendering brighter or darker, cooler or warmer, and more gray or more intense.

Figure 4–12

- Once you adjust the exposure, the Autodesk Revit software remembers the settings for the current view the next time you repeat the rendering process.

Display

The *Display* area in the Rendering dialog box presents a button for **Show the model** when a rendering is active or **Show the rendering** when a rendering has been saved to the view. If it's grayed out, it means no rendering has been done in the active view.

Hint: Saving Custom Rendering Settings

If you have modified the rendering settings quality, you can save the settings to a view template, which can be used in another view or project.

1. Set up the 3D view with the rendering settings. Only 3D views display Render Settings.
2. Right-click on the view name in the Project Browser and select **Create View Template From View...**.
3. Enter a new name for the view template and click **OK**.
4. In the View Templates dialog box (shown in Figure 4–13), verify that the *Render Settings* are correct.

Figure 4–13

5. Click OK.

- To use the view settings for another view in the current project, right-click on the view name in the Project Browser and select **Apply Template Properties**.

- To use the view settings in another project, in the *Manage* tab>Settings panel, click (Transfer Project Standards). You must be in a plan view to transfer the standards.

Practice 4a | Produce Basic Renderings

Practice Objectives

- Render a region of a view in Draft mode to test the materials.
- Modify materials and render at Medium mode.

In this practice, you will set up and render a test region of a view. You will also modify the materials of some elements and test the rendering again at a slightly higher quality.

Task 1 - Render a region of the view.

1. In the practice files folder, open **Midrise-Rendering-M.rvt**.

2. Open the 3D Views: **Front Perspective** view.

3. Set the *Visual Style* to ⬚ (Shaded) to see the materials that come with the element styles (such as the brick walls, glass curtain wall and windows, and grass on the site), as shown in Figure 4–14.

Your view might look slightly different.

Figure 4–14

4. In the View Control Bar, click ☁ (Show Rendering Dialog).

5. In the Rendering dialog box, select **Region**. Modify the region in the view so it is similar to Figure 4–15.

Figure 4–15

6. Set the following options in the Rendering dialog box:

- *Quality:* **Draft**
- *Output Settings:* **Screen**
- *Lighting:* **Exterior: Sun only**
- *Background:* Sky: **Few Clouds**

7. Click **Render**.

Task 2 - Modify materials and render the view again.

---

1. Using the Draft quality setting displays the materials, but is not clear enough to provide a good view of the building, especially the mullions of the curtain wall. However, you can see that the stairs are made of brick, where they should be showing a stone material.

2. Click **Show the model** to return to the unrendered perspective. Keep the Rendering dialog box open and move it off to the side.

3. Select the stairs. In Properties, click ⊞ (Edit Type).

4. Set the *Tread*, *Riser*, and *Stringer Material* for the stairs to **Masonry-Stone**, as shown in Figure 4–16.

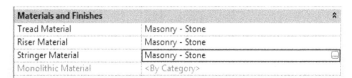

Materials and Finishes		⌃
Tread Material	Masonry - Stone	
Riser Material	Masonry - Stone	
Stringer Material	Masonry - Stone	…
Monolithic Material	<By Category>	

Figure 4–16

5. Click **OK** to close the Type Properties dialog box.

6. In the Rendering dialog box, set the *Quality Setting* to **Medium** and click **Render**.

7. The stairs display the correct color and the medium setting displays the curtain wall mullions more precisely, as shown in Figure 4–17.

8. Click on **Adjust Exposure...** and adjust the exposure to brighten the rendering.

Figure 4–17

9. Save the rendering to the project as **Entry-Medium**.

10. Save the project and keep it open for the next practice.

4.2 Working with Lighting

A crucial component of rendering is setting up lights —both sunlight and light fixtures that radiate light, as shown in Figure 4–18. Sunlight is controlled by the location, time of day, and cloud cover. Artificial light comes from lighting components that are added to the reflected ceiling plan or floor plan.

Figure 4–18

Light Fixture Families

Light fixtures are families that are placed with (Component). Many of the light fixture families included with Autodesk Revit have multiple options for the type of lamp in the fixture, as shown in Figure 4–19.

Figure 4–19

Viewing Light Sources

As you place light fixtures, especially spotlights, sconces, or downlights illuminating specific objects, it is helpful to toggle on the light sources, as shown in Figure 4–20.

Figure 4–20

How To: Toggle On Light Sources

1. Open the Visibility/Graphic Overrides dialog box.
2. In the *Model Categories* tab, expand **Lighting Fixtures** and select **Light Source**, as shown in Figure 4–21.

Figure 4–21

3. Click **OK**.

* Toggle on the ⬜ (Shaded) visual style to get the best view of the light sources. Shading displays the difference between the beam angle and the field angle for spotlights.

* To have even more accurate lighting in a rendering, you can specify photometric light sources. These sources use an IES file from the lighting manufacturer. This file describes the light intensity for points on a spherical grid and how the light comes from the fixture. Light sources are specified in the lighting fixture family.

Setting Up Light Groups

While a project might include hundreds of light fixtures in the building, only some of them impact the rendering you are working on. To save time, limit the light fixtures to those that are used in the current view by creating and setting up light groups.

How To: Create Light Groups

1. Open the view that displays the lights you want to group.
2. Select at least one of the lights.
3. In the Options Bar, in the Light Group drop-down list, select **Edit/New...** to create a new group, as shown in Figure 4–22.

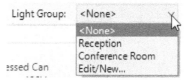

Figure 4–22

4. The Artificial Lights dialog box opens, as shown in Figure 4–23.

Figure 4–23

5. In the *Group Options* area in the dialog box, click **New** to create a new group.
6. In the New Light Group dialog box, enter a name for the light group and click **OK**.
7. Select the new group name and in the *Group Options* area, click **Edit...**

8. The floating Light Group panel displays. Select 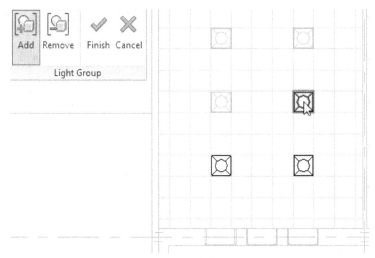 (Add) and click on each light that you want to add to the light group, as shown in Figure 4–24.

Figure 4–24

9. Click ✓ (Finish), then click **OK**.

• When you need to edit a light group, select at least one light. In the Options Bar, select a light group from the Light Group drop-down list (as shown in Figure 4–25) and click **Edit...**.

Figure 4–25

• If you select a light that is already part of another group, you will get the message that you are about to move the light to a new group, as shown in Figure 4–26.

Figure 4–26

How To: Add Lights to a Light Group

1. Open the view that displays the lights you want to add to a group.
2. Select at least one of the lights.
3. In the Options Bar, in the Light Group drop-down list, select an existing group.
4. An alert box opens prompting you that you are about to move the selected light(s) to a new light group. Click **OK** or **Cancel**.

How To: Use Light Groups in a Rendering

1. Open a 3D view to render. In the View Control Bar, click
   (Show Rendering Dialog).
2. In the Rendering dialog box, in the *Lighting* area, select a *Scheme* that includes artificial lights.
3. Click **Artificial Lights...**.
4. In the Artificial Lights dialog box for the view, the lists of grouped and ungrouped lights display. Clear the groups and ungrouped lights that you do not need for the rendering, as shown in Figure 4–27.

This option is only available if a Scheme with artificial lights has been selected.

Figure 4–27

- You can also dim a light or light group using this dialog box. Set the value for *Dimming* to either **0** (off) or **1** (not dimmed).

Hint: Section Boxes and Rendering

Section boxes are another way to limit the geometry viewed and calculated when creating a rendering.

In a 3D view, in the *Extents* area in the Properties dialog box, click **Section Box**. The default size is the extents of the view. Resize the section box using the controls, as shown in Figure 4–28, before rendering the view.

Figure 4–28

Practice 4b | Work with Lighting

Practice Objectives

- Set up light groups for a specific room and add light fixtures.
- Render a view using light groups.

In this practice, you will set up light groups, add a light fixture, view the light source, and render a region. Once the rendering is finished, you will adjust the exposure, as shown in Figure 4–29.

Original rendering   *Exposure adjusted*

Figure 4–29

Task 1 - Set up light groups.

1. Continue working in **Midrise-Rendering-M.rvt**.

2. Open the Ceiling Plans: **Level 1** view. Some light fixtures have been added to the project, as shown in Figure 4–30.

Figure 4–30

3. Zoom in on the Reception Room in the lower left corner of the building (as shown in Figure 4–30).

4. Select one of the lights. In the Options Bar, in the Light Group drop-down list, select **Edit/New**.

5. In the Artificial Lights dialog box, in the *Group Options* area, click **New**. Set the name to **Reception Room** and click **OK**. Click **OK** to close the dialog box.

6. Select all six lights in the Reception Room and set the *Light Group* to **Reception Room**, as shown in Figure 4–31.

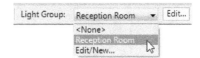

Figure 4–31

7. Click **OK** to move the lights to the Reception Room light group. Click in an empty space in the view to clear the selection of the lights.

Task 2 - Add light fixtures.

1. Open the Floor Plans: **Level 1** view and zoom in on the Reception room.

2. In the *Architecture* tab>Build panel, click (Component).

3. In the *Modify | Place Component* tab>Mode panel, click (Load Family).

4. In the Load Family dialog box, navigate to the practice files *Families* folder, select **M_Floor Lamp - Arm Extension.rfa**, and load it into the project.

5. Place the lamp behind the chairs near the outside corner of the wall. Rotate it as shown in Figure 4–32.

Figure 4–32

6. Select the floor lamp. In the Options Bar, set the *Light Group* to **Reception Room**. Click **OK** to accept moving the light to the Reception Room light group.

7. Open the **3D Views: Interior Perspective** view.

8. View the light sources. Enter **VG** and expand the *Lighting Fixtures* category. Select **Light Source** and click **OK**.

9. In the View Status Bar, click (Shaded). The light sources display similar to those shown in Figure 4–33, depending on the floor lamp you selected.

Figure 4–33

Task 3 - Render a view.

1. In the View Control Bar, click ☜ (Show Rendering Dialog).

2. In the Rendering dialog box, in the *Lighting* area, set the *Scheme* to **Interior: Sun and Artificial**.

3. Beside *Sun Setting*, click ⌐…⌐ (Choose a sun location).

4. In the Sun Settings dialog box, *Solar Study* area, select **Still**.

5. In the *Settings* area, set the *Time* to early morning. This keeps the light coming in from the windows from being too bright. Click **OK**.

6. In the Rendering dialog box, click the **Artificial Lights...** button.

7. In the Artificial Lights dialog box, verify that **Reception Room** is toggled on and **Ungrouped Lights** is cleared so that they do not display in the rendering, as shown in Figure 4–34.

Figure 4–34

8. Click **OK**.

9. In the Rendering dialog box, select **Region**. Modify the region so that it shows the floor lamp and some other light fixture.

10. Set the *Quality Setting* to **Draft** and click **Render**.

11. When the Rendering Progress dialog box opens, check the number of Artificial Lights it is calculating, as shown in Figure 4–35.

Figure 4–35

12. When the rendering displays, click **Adjust Exposure...** and modify the various exposure controls, then click **Apply** to see the changes. Click **Reset** to go back to the original settings. Close the Rendering dialog box.

13. Save the project and keep it open for the next practice.

4.3 Enhancing Renderings

Many components provided in the Autodesk Revit software are ready to be rendered. Although furniture has a specific wood pattern, lights include light sources, and windows have transparent glass material in the panes, this is often not enough. You can further enhance renderings by splitting faces and applying different materials to elements such as walls and floors. You can also add Rich Photorealistic Content (RPC) components, such as trees and people, that are specifically created for adding to renderings, as shown in Figure 4–36.

Figure 4–36

Applying Materials

You may want to apply information that is not in the model element, such as different materials on the face of a wall, as shown in Figure 4–37. The **Split Face** command divides an element face into smaller separate faces. You can then use the **Paint** command to apply different materials to the faces.

Figure 4–37

- The changes made with **Split Face** and **Paint** are displayed in elevations and 3D views.

- **Split Face** and **Paint** do not alter the structure of the wall.

- The area and other information about the materials can be used in a Material takeoff schedule.

How To: Create a Split Face

1. Switch to an elevation view (a 3D view works as well).

2. In the *Modify* tab>Geometry panel, click ⬠ (Split Face).

3. Select the edge of the face that you want to modify. Use <Tab> to toggle through the available faces.

4. In the *Modify | Split Face>Create Boundary* tab>Draw panel, use the sketch tools to create a sketch to define the split, as shown in Figure 4–38.

If the ⬚ (Select elements by face) option is toggled on in the lower left corner of the Status Bar, you can click directly on the face.

Figure 4–38

- The split must be a closed shape completely inside the face, or an open shape that touches the face edges.
- Windows are cut out of faces automatically.

5. Click ✓ (Finish Edit Mode).

- Before you begin working with split faces, ensure that the walls are mitered. By default, the walls are butted to each other. This creates a problem when you select faces.

- To save time, use a wall style that includes the primary material you want to use on the split face. For example, if you are working with brick, set the wall to a type that has a brick face. This way, you can work with the brick courses when creating the split face.

- When using a material, such as brick, you can snap to the pattern and even lock the split lines to the pattern, as shown in Figure 4–39.

Figure 4–39

You can double-click on the edge of the split face lines to switch to the Edit Boundary mode. If you double-click on the wall face (with the **Select elements by face** option toggled on) it switches to the Edit Profile mode, which impacts the entire wall, not just the split face boundary.

How To: Apply Material with Paint

1. In the *Modify* tab>Geometry panel, click (Paint) or enter **PT**.
2. In the Material Browser, select a material. You can run a search or filter the list using specific types of materials, as shown in Figure 4–40.

The browser remains open as you apply the paint.

Material Browser - Acoustic Ceiling Tile 24 x 24   ?   X

Search

Project Materials: All ▼

<All>
Carpet
Concrete
Gas
Generic   Table Top   Teak   Textile -
Glass   Black
Masonry
Metal
Miscellaneous
Paint
Plastic
System   Textile -   Tile, Mosaic, Tile,
Textile   Slate Blue   Gray   Porce..., 4in
Unassigned
Wood

Figure 4–40

3. Hover the cursor over the face you want to paint. It should highlight, as shown in Figure 4–41. Click on the face to apply the material.

Figure 4–41

4. Continue selecting materials and painting other faces if needed.
5. In the Material Browser, click **Done** to finish the command.

- Some material patterns display as shaded when you zoom out. Zoom in to display the pattern. Other material patterns only display when you are in the ⬛ (Realistic) visual style or when you render.

- To remove the material applied to a face, in the *Modify* tab> Geometry panel, expand ⬛ (Paint) and click ⬛ (Remove Paint). Select the face(s) from which you want to remove the material.

Adding People and Other Components

Rich Photorealistic Content (RPC) is a specific type of component that helps to make renderings more lifelike. The Autodesk Revit libraries include RPC people and plants, as shown in Figure 4–42, as well as office items and vehicles. To place signs, paintings, and other flat graphics such as the picture in Figure 4–42, you can add decals.

Figure 4–42

Adding RPC elements

RPC elements are added using the **Component** command. Samples of vehicles, people, and office objects are available in the Autodesk Revit Library in the *Entourage* folder. Once you load them into the project, you can select them from the Type Selector, as shown in Figure 4–43.

You can purchase additional objects from .ArchVision™

Figure 4–43

- You need to be in a 3D orthographic view or floor plan view to place components.

In a plan, the person displays with a point indicating the direction in which they are facing. In a 3D view, they display in outline. In a rendering, they display as they have been created, as shown in Figure 4–44.

RPC components

Figure 4–44

- If you are working with Autodesk Revit topography element components such as trees and shrubs, you can use a different command that places the element directly on the toposurface. In the *Massing & Site* tab>Model Site panel, click 🌲 (Site Component).

Adding Decals

Decals are links to images that you can place on flat or cylindrical surfaces. They are used for signs, pictures, or other flat surfaced elements. Decals display an outline in most visual styles (as shown in Figure 4–45); however, they display in full when rendered or in the Realistic visual style, as shown in Figure 4–46.

Figure 4–45

Figure 4–46

How To: Create a Decal Type

1. Start the **Decal** command.
   - If no decal exists in the project, the Decal Types dialog box will open. Click ⬚ (Create New Decal), set a name for it, and skip to step 6.
2. In the Type Selector, select a Decal and click **Edit Type**.
3. In the Type Properties dialog box, click **Duplicate...**.
4. In the Name dialog box, enter a name for the decal and click **OK**.
5. Beside the **Decal Attributes** parameter, click **Edit...**
6. In the Decal Types dialog box beside *Source*, click ⬚.

If you are adding the first decal in a project, you will work in the full Decal Types dialog box.

7. In the Select File dialog box, select the image and click **Open**. The new image displays and you can modify the other settings, as shown in Figure 4–47.

Figure 4–47

8. Click **OK**.

- To open the full Decal Types dialog box, in the *Insert* tab>Link panel, expand (Decal) and click (Decal Types).

How To: Add Decals

1. Open a 2D view such as a section or elevation.

2. In the *Insert* tab>Link panel, expand (Decal) and click (Place Decal).

3. In the Type Selector, select from the loaded decals.
4. Place the decal on the face of an element.

5. In the Options Bar, specify the *Width* and *Height*. Click **Lock Proportions** to lock the aspect ratio of the decal, as shown in Figure 4–48. Click **Reset** to return to the original size.

| Modify | Decal | Width: 604 | Height 610 | ☑ Lock Proportions | Reset |

Figure 4–48

- You can also use the *Drag* controls to resize the decal.

Practice 4c | Enhance Renderings

Practice Objectives

- Modify the floor materials by splitting the face and painting a new material on part of it.
- Add a decal to a surface.
- Add people and plant components in a room and render it.

In this practice, you will split the face of the floor and apply a different material to a part of it. You will also add a sign to the reception desk and add people and trees. You will then render it, as shown in Figure 4–49.

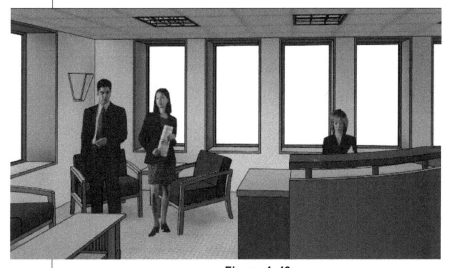

Figure 4–49

Task 1 - Modify the floor material.

1. Continue working in **Midrise-Rendering-M.rvt**.

2. Open the **Floor Plans: Level 1** view.

3. Zoom in on the reception room in the lower left part of the building.

4. In the *Modify | Floors* tab>Geometry panel, click 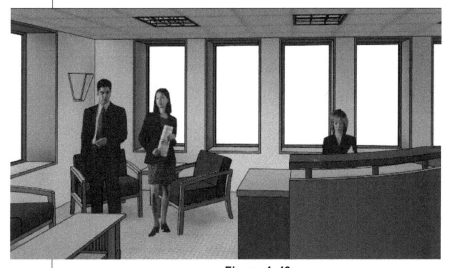 (Split Face.

5. Hover the cursor over the interior edge of one of the exterior walls and select the floor.

6. In the *Modify | Split Face>Create Boundary* tab>Draw panel, use the draw tools to split the reception room floor into two faces, as shown in Figure 4–50. Click ✓ (Finish Edit Mode) when you are done.

The sketch must be closed or touch existing boundary lines to make the closed shape.

Figure 4–50

7. Set the *Visual Style* to **Realistic**. The existing floor type is carpet.

8. In the *Modify* tab>Geometry panel, click 🖺 (Paint).

9. In the Material Browser, select a material for part of the floor. A variety of carpet styles are available in the project. There are also a number of *Wood* project materials that you can chose from, as shown in Figure 4–51. The flooring will update in real time with the material you select, as shown in Figure 4–52.

Figure 4–51   **Figure 4–52**

10. Click **Done**.

   • If you want to change the other half of the flooring and keep the Paint command from changing the rest of the carpeting in the building, you need to create a second split face.

11. Open the **Interior Perspective** view and test out the flooring change by setting the *Visual Style* to **Realistic**. Turn off the light source.

   • Adjust the Graphic Display Options as needed.

12. Modify the view angle, if needed, to show the floor.

13. Save the project.

Task 2 - Add a decal.

1. Return to the **Floor Plans: Level 1** view.

2. Add a section that will display the double doors to the right of the reception desk.

3. Modify the section cut plane if needed, as shown in Figure 4–53.

Figure 4–53

4. Open the section view, adjust the crop region (as shown in Figure 4–54), and set the *Detail Level* to **Fine**.

Figure 4–54

5. In the *Insert* tab>Link panel, click (Decal).

6. In the Decal Types dialog box, click (Create New Decal) and name it **Conference Room Sign**.

7. In the Select File dialog box, navigate to the practice files *Images* folder and select **Conference Room Sign.png**. Click **Open**. The new image displays and you can modify the other settings, as shown in Figure 4–55.

Figure 4–55

8. Place the sign on the face of the wall.

9. Click ⬦ (Modify) and select the new decal.

10. In the Options Bar, verify that **Lock Proportions** is selected. Change the *Height* to **300mm**.

11. Click in the *Width* edit box to apply the change.

12. Change the *Visual Style* to **Realistic** to see the final image. Move the decal where you want it on the wall, such as that shown in Figure 4–56.

Figure 4–56

13. Save the project.

Task 3 - Add people and plants.

---

1. Return to the **Floor Plans: Level 1** view.

2. Change the *Visual Style* to Hidden Line.

3. In the *Architecture* tab>Build panel, click ⬛ (Component).

4. In the *Modify | Place Component* tab>Mode panel, click ⬛ (Load Family).

Note that in the Load Family dialog box, you can access the Autodesk Revit Library by clicking on the Imperial or Metric Library folder in the Places panel.

5. In the practice files *Families* folder, select **M_RCP Male.rfa** and **M_RCP Female.rfa** and load them into the project. In the Autodesk Revit Library *Planting* folder, select and load **M_RCP Tree - Conifer.rfa** and **M_RCP Tree - Deciduous.rfa**.

You can work in the Realistic visual style or set the view back to Hidden Line.

6. Place several people inside the Reception Room in the floor plan. Rotate them as required. The pointed end is the front of the person, as shown in Figure 4–57.

Entourage : RPC Male : Dwayne

Figure 4–57

There is a toposurface in this project.

7. In the *Massing & Site* tab>Model Site panel, click 🌲 (Site Component).

8. Add trees outside the windows so that they can be seen in the perspective view.

9. Switch to the **Interior Perspective** view. You should see outlines of the people and possibly some of the trees through the window, similar to that shown in Figure 4–58.

Figure 4–58

10. Switch to the ⬦ (Realistic) visual style to test the direction of the people.

11. Render a region or, if time permits, the entire scene.

12. Save and close the project.

Chapter Review Questions

1. What should you do to prepare a view for rendering?

   a. Toggle on the **Sun Path**.

   b. Lock the view.

   c. Add lights.

   d. Set the *Visual Style* to (Realistic).

2. What is the purpose of the **Region** option in the Rendering dialog box, as shown in Figure 4–59?

   Figure 4–59

   a. It only toggles on lights in a specified region.

   b. It only displays materials in a specified region.

   c. It only includes shadows in a specified region.

   d. It only renders in a specified region.

3. If a rendering is darker than expected, how do you make it lighter?

   a. Add more light fixtures.

   b. Adjust the exposure.

   c. Modify the location of the sun.

   d. Change the *Lighting Scheme*.

4. How do you limit the number of lights used in a rendering?

   a. Hide any lights that you do not want to use.

   b. Isolate the lights that you want to use.

   c. Set up a light group.

   d. Delete the additional lights.

5. How can you display the light sources?

   a. Set the *Visual Style* to **Shaded**.

   b. In the Visibility/Graphic Overrides dialog box, select **Light Source**.

   c. In Properties, select **Light Source**.

   d. It depends on the type of light fixture family used.

Command Summary

Button	Command	Location
	Component	• **Ribbon:** *Architecture* tab>Build panel • **Shortcut:** CM
	Decal Types	• **Ribbon:** *Insert* tab>Link panel, expand Decal
	Load Family	• **Ribbon:** *Modify	Place Component* tab>Mode panel
	Place Decal	• **Ribbon:** *Insert* tab>Link panel, expand Decal
	Site Component	• **Ribbon:** *Massing & Site* tab>Model Site panel
	Show Rendering Dialog	• **View Control Bar**
	Transfer Project Standards	• **Ribbon:** *Manage* tab>Settings panel

Additional Tools for Massing

There are many other tools available in the Autodesk® Revit® software that can be used when creating massing studies for your models. This appendix provides details about tools and commands that are related to those covered in this guide.

Learning Objectives in This Appendix

- Review the process of creating a conceptual mass family, including dimensions, labels, and Family Types.
- Work with reference-based forms.

A.1 Conceptual Mass Families

Conceptual mass families can be used to create massing studies that can then be used in a project. This is useful if you are creating multiple copies of one building design on a site, as shown in Figure A–1. As with other families, you can use reference planes, dimensions and labels, and types to make the mass elements parametric.

Figure A–1

How To: Create a Conceptual Mass Family

1. In the Home screen *Families* area, click **New...**, or in the *File* tab, expand ⬜ (New) and click ⬛ (Conceptual Mass).
2. In the New Conceptual Mass - Select Template File dialog box, in the *Conceptual Mass* folder, select the **Metric Mass.rft** template and click **Open**.
3. In the Conceptual Mass Environment, in the *Create* tab> Draw panel (shown in Figure A–2), add reference planes, reference lines, dimensions, labels, and other parameters.
4. Use the drawing tools to draw the profiles and paths that will make up the solid.

Figure A–2

5. Select the sketched linework.

6. In the *Modify | Lines* tab>Form panel, click (Create Form). The Autodesk Revit software creates a 3D mass based on the selected linework.
7. Use the dimensioning tools to add additional labels, as shown in Figure A–3.

Figure A–3

8. In the *Modify* tab>Properties panel, click (Family Types). In the Family Types dialog box (shown in Figure A–4), set up formulas, additional parameters, and Family Types.

Figure A–4

9. Click (Save).

- In the Family Editor panel, you can click 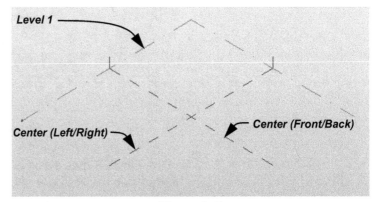 (Load into Project) to load the new mass into an open project.

- Information about creating sketches and forms is covered in *Chapter 1: Massing Studies*.

- The conceptual mass family template contains one level and two reference planes, as shown in Figure A–5.

You can click on the edge of the levels or reference planes to set the work plane.

Level 1

Center (Left/Right)

Center (Front/Back)

Figure A–5

- To select another level by default, open its plan view. Alternatively, select the level marker in a 3D view, as shown in Figure A–6.

Levels : Level : Level 3

Figure A–6

- The background of 3D views in the conceptual mass family file displays as a light gray gradient.

Reference Based Forms

If you want an extruded form or a sweep to retain its shape along the path when the related parameters are flexed, you can make the profile lines a reference. Select the profile lines as though you are going to make a form. Before selecting the Form command, in Properties, in the *Identity Data* category, select **Is Reference Line**.

Before you set the profile as a reference, the lines display as shown in Figure A–7.

Figure A–7

Once you have set them as a reference, the Properties change and you see reference planes along the edges of the profile, as shown in Figure A–8.

Figure A–8

Practice A1 | Advanced Conceptual Massing

Practice Objectives

- Create reference planes and dimension and label them.
- Create a mass form using reference lines.
- Insert the mass family into a project and place instances of it using different parameters.

In this practice, you will create a conceptual mass family with dimensions and parameters, as shown in Figure A–9. You will then place two copies of the mass family into a project and modify them using the parameters set up in the mass family, as shown in Figure A–10.

- This practice requires an understanding of conceptual massing and parametric family concepts.

Figure A–9

Figure A–10

Task 1 - Create the base parametric framework.

1. In the *File* tab, expand (New) and select ▭ (Conceptual Mass).

2. In the New Conceptual Mass - Select Template File dialog box, select the **Metric Mass.rft** template from the Revit Family Template, Conceptual Mass folder, and click **Open**.

3. Save the family as **M-Edmon-Towers-Model.rfa**.

4. Verify that you are in the **3D Views: {3D}** view and that no other views are open.

5. Open the **Floor Plans: Level 1** view.

6. Enter **WT** to tile the two views and then **ZA** to fit the view in the windows.

7. Working in the 3D view, in the *Create* tab>Draw panel, click (Reference Plane).

8. In the Options Bar, set the *Placement Plane* to **Level: Level 1.**

9. Draw the four reference planes shown in Figure A–11. The two angled reference planes should be at different angles.

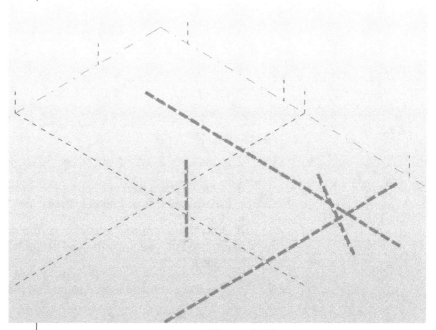

Figure A–11

10. In the plan view, dimension the horizontal and vertical reference planes, label them (instance parameters), and set the values, as shown in Figure A–12.

11. Move the angled lines, if needed, to fit inside the footprint of the building. Dimension, but do not label them. Select the reference plane and set the values, as shown in Figure A–12.

Flexing the angles creates additional complexity. Once the rest of the mass works as expected, you can try adding labels and flexing the angles.

Figure A–12

12. In the *Create* tab>Draw panel, click (Reference Line).

13. In the Options Bar, verify that *Placement Plane* is still set to **Level: Level 1** and select **Chain**.

14. Draw the reference lines shown above in Figure A–12. Ensure that you snap to the intersections of the reference planes.

15. Flex the width and length to ensure that everything works.

16. Save the family.

Task 2 - Create levels and additional profiles.

Remember that levels in massing families are not the same as levels in projects. These are for setting heights.

1. Open the **Elevations: South** view.

2. Add two levels and dimension and label them (instance parameters), as shown in Figure A–13. The exact height does not matter at this time.

Figure A–13

3. In the *Create* tab>Properties panel, click (Family Types).

4. Add a formula to the *Half Height* parameter as shown in Figure A–14. Set the *Height* parameter to **46000** and click **OK**.

Figure A–14

5. Open the **Floor Plans: Level 2** view.

6. Add two reference planes, then dimension them, label them (instance parameters), and set the values, as shown in Figure A–15.

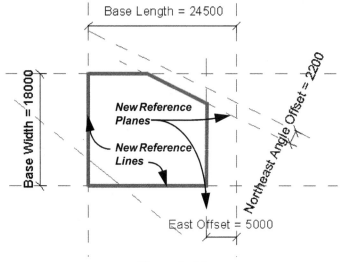

Figure A–15

7. Add reference lines on the *Placement Plane:* **Level: Level 2** using the boundary shown above in Figure A–15.

8. Flex the parameters to ensure that they work.

9. Open the **Floor Plans: Level 3** view.

10. Add the reference plane, label, and reference line boundary, as shown in Figure A–16.

Figure A–16

11. Flex the parameters to test the framework.

12. Save the family.

Task 3 - Create a mass form.

1. Open the default 3D view and select the three profiles made of reference lines that should be similar to Figure A–17.

2. In the *Modify | Reference Lines* tab>Form panel, click

   (Create Form). A new mass element should display, as shown in Figure A–18.

Figure A–17	Figure A–18

3. Use the Family Types dialog box to flex the parameters.

4. While in this dialog box, verify that all of the parameters are Instance parameters so they can be modified in a project easily. They should have (default) after the parameter name.

   • If they are not, you can change them one at a time by

     selecting a parameter and clicking 🖉 (Edit Parameter) to change it to an Instance parameter.

5. In 3D view with nothing selected, clear the check from **Work Plane-Based** in Properties.

6. Save the family.

Task 4 - Use the mass family in a project.

1. Open the project **Edmon-Towers-Study-M.rvt**.

2. Switch back to the mass family file and load it into the project.

3. Close the alert box.

4. Place two mass families in the new site location, as shown in Figure A–19.

Mass families can be placed using the **Component** *or* **Place Mass** *commands.*

Figure A–19

5. Select one of the mass family elements and in Properties, modify the various dimensions so that the buildings are different.

   • If prompted with a warning suggesting that the type cannot be created, cancel and use a different dimension.

6. Save the project.

Command Summary

Button	Command	Location
	Conceptual Mass	• **Ribbon:** *File* tab>New
	Create Form	• **Family Editor Ribbon:** *Modify | Place Lines* tab> Form panel
	Family Types	• **Family Editor Ribbon:** *Create* or *Modify* tab> Properties panel
	Load into Project	• **Family Editor Ribbon:** All tabs> Family Editor panel
	Load into Project and Close	• **Family Editor Ribbon:** All tabs> Family Editor panel
	Place Mass	• **Ribbon:** *Massing & Site* tab> Conceptual Mass panel

Additional Tools for Rendering

There are many other tools available in the Autodesk® Revit® software that can be used when creating stunning visual aids of your models, like enhanced materials and walkthroughs. This appendix provides details about tools and commands that are related to those covered in this guide.

Learning Objectives in This Appendix

- Create materials and material libraries that can be used in multiple projects.
- Create and edit a perspective walkthrough.

B.1 Creating Materials

When you shade or render Autodesk Revit models, their appearance depends on the materials that have been associated with the elements, as shown in a shaded view in Figure B–1. Materials also include information that can be used in material takeoff schedules and in energy and structural analysis. You can use materials supplied with the Autodesk Revit software or create custom materials.

Figure B–1

- Materials can be assigned in several ways: using ⊕□ (Paint) on faces, setting it in the layers of system families (such as walls and floors), and in object styles. You also assign materials when you create other component families, such as doors and furniture.

Materials consist of 2D graphic settings for shading, surface, and cut patterns and the 3D rendering appearance, as well as physical and thermal properties. You can also include identity data, such as manufacturer, model, and keynotes.

Material Libraries

Materials are stored in libraries, which can be shared between Autodesk Revit projects and the AutoCAD, Autodesk® Inventor®, Showcase and Autodesk® 3ds Max® software. Before creating custom materials it is recommended that you create a custom library. Materials can be copied between the current project and the library.

- You can also use Transfer Project Standards to bring in all the materials from another project into the current project.

- Within the Material Libraries toolbar, you can sort the material libraries (as shown in Figure B–2) and view the material with different sizes for better viewing capabilities (as shown in Figure B–3).

Figure B–2

Figure B–3

- Older versions of materials may need to be updated with appearance assets, as shown in Figure B–4. All legacy materials still work but they may not be as complex and nuanced when rendering.

Figure B–4

How To: Create a Material Library

1. In the *Manage* tab>Settings panel, click (Materials).

2. At the bottom of the Material Browser, expand (Creates, opens and edits user-defined libraries) and select **Create New Library**, as shown in Figure B–5.

Figure B–5

3. In the Select File dialog box, navigate to the appropriate folder, type a *File name* and save the library. The Material Library displays in the Library list without any materials displayed.

4. Create new materials in the current project. Then drag and drop both new and existing materials from the project materials into the new library, as shown in Figure B–6.

Libraries that come with the Autodesk Revit software are locked. You can copy materials from them but cannot add or change materials in them.

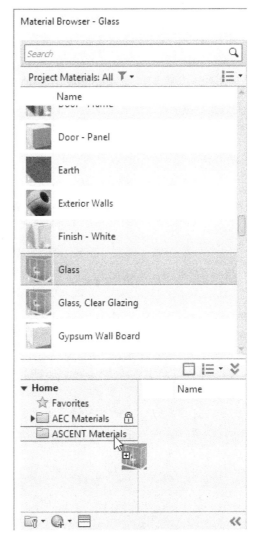

Figure B–6

How To: Create a Material

1. In the *Manage* tab>Settings panel, click ⬡ (Materials).

2. In the Material Editor, expand 🔄 (Creates or duplicates a material), and select either **Create New Material** or **Duplicate Material** as shown in Figure B–7. If you are duplicating a material, select an existing material similar to what you want to use first.

*You can also right-click on an existing material in the Material Browser and select **Duplicate**.*

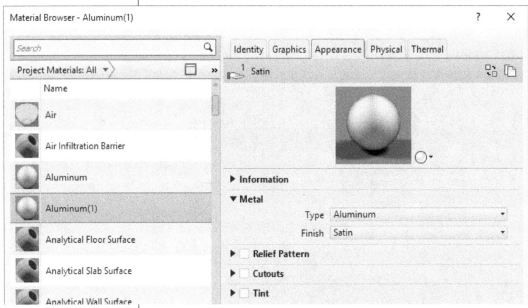

Figure B–7

3. A new material is added to the current project. Modify the name of the material or right-click on the Material name in the Material Browser and select **Rename**.

   • Duplicated materials include all of the properties of the existing material as shown for a new Aluminum material in Figure B–8.

Figure B–8

4. Fill out the information on each of the tabs.
5. Click **Apply** and add additional materials.
6. Click **OK** when you are finished.

Identity Tab

In the *Identity* tab, you set up the *Descriptive Information*, *Product Information*, and *Revit Annotation Information* for the material, as shown in Figure B–9. This information can be used in material takeoff schedules.

Figure B–9

Graphics Tab

In the *Graphics* tab (shown in Figure B–10), you set how a material displays in shaded or hidden line mode. The Surface and Cut Patterns can be set for Foreground and Background.

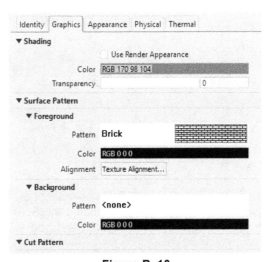

Figure B–10

- The *Shading* area controls how the material displays when an element is shaded. If you want the shaded view to resemble the rendered view, select **Use Render Appearance**. The color and other options are modified to match the Render Appearance selection. Alternatively, you can set up a color and transparency ratio. Only use this if the render appearance would be too dark or otherwise not suit the use.

The *Surface Pattern* and *Cut Pattern* areas enable you to select a fill pattern and color to display on a surface or in a section cut. Surface patterns stay true to size. Cut patterns are drafting patterns, which change size according to the view scale.

Appearance Tab

In the *Appearance* tab, you can set different aspects of a rendered material, including **Information**, the type of material (in this example Masonry is selected, as shown in Figure B–11) and other parameters depending on the type of material you are working with. Note that changing the asset changes all of the information, so check if that is an option first.

Figure B–11

- You can select how to display the preview of the material by expanding the Scene list next to the graphic, as shown in Figure B–11 above.

- You can modify the *Render Settings* of the preview to either **Draft Quality** or **Production Quality**.

- If you duplicate a material and then change asset-related information (such as the Image or Color) the original material also updates. To prevent this from happening, duplicate or change the asset before making changes.

Physical Tab

In the *Physical* tab, you can specify information about the physical properties of the material. The options vary by material type, as shown in Figure B–12.

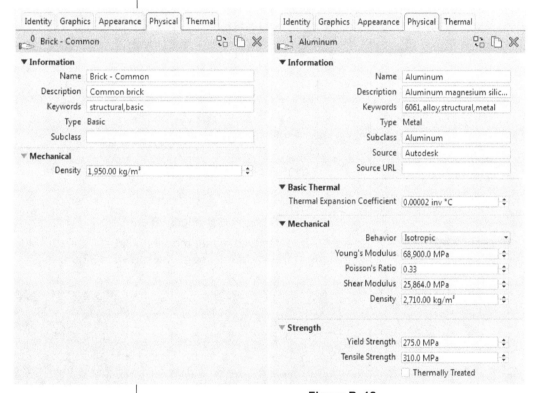

Figure B–12

- Some materials, such as **EPDM Membrane** or **Vapor Retarder**, do not have physical properties, but do have thermal properties.

- Analytical surface and Default materials do not have physical or thermal properties.

- As changing the asset changes all of the information, you should check to see if that is an option first.

Working with Assets

Physical assets contain preset parameters for materials. These assets are available in the *Appearance*, *Physical* and *Thermal* tabs. Autodesk provides an extensive library of assets that are divided by material type, as shown in Figure B–13. You can modify and add assets to materials depending on the variables required in the project.

Figure B–13

Assets updated with higher rendering capabilities do not have a triangle in the lower left corner, as shown in Figure B–14.

Original Cherry asset

Updated Cherry asset

Figure B–14

How To: Replace an Asset for a Material

1. In the Material Browser, select the material that you want to modify.
2. Duplicate the material and give it a name indicating it's the new asset for the material. NOTE: If you replace an asset or material with the new asset, the old one will no longer be available to use.
3. In the *Appearance*, *Physical*, or *Thermal* tab, click

   □⁺⃗
   ⬚ (Replaces this asset).
4. In the Asset Browser, hover the cursor over the required

   asset and click ⇄ (Replaces the current asset in the editor with this asset), as shown in Figure B–15.

Figure B–15

5. Close the Asset Browser.

• The assets are filtered by type. Therefore, you need to modify the Appearance asset by clicking through the *Appearance* tab, etc.

• You can create new assets by duplicating an existing one and then modifying the parameters.

B.2 Creating Walkthroughs

A *walkthrough* is a series of perspective views linked together in a path. You specify the location of *key frames*—specific points in the plan that create the path of the walkthrough. Key frames are displayed as squares on the path, as shown in Figure B–16. A line shows the view direction. Once you create a walkthrough, you can edit its individual frames and export the whole sequence to an AVI file.

Figure B–16

How To: Create a Walkthrough

1. Open a plan view. Walkthroughs can be made in other views, but they are typically laid out in plan views.
2. In the *View* tab>Create panel (or Quick Access Toolbar),

   expand ⬙ (3D View) and click 👣 (Walkthrough).
3. In the Options Bar, set the perspective and offset from the level, as shown in Figure B–17.

Figure B–17

4. Click on the screen to place the first key frame.
5. Continue adding key frames. You can change the offset if required. For example, if you are walking up a set of stairs.
6. In the *Modify | Walkthrough* tab>Walkthrough panel, click

    (Finish Walkthrough). A walkthrough view is created in the Project Browser with the default name of **Walkthrough1**.

•   You can view and modify the walkthrough in either the plan view (to edit the path) or walkthrough view (to display the 3D views).

How To: View a Walkthrough

*To see the camera and path in a plan view, right-click on the walkthrough name in the Walkthrough section of the Project Browser and select **Show Camera**.*

1. In the Project Browser, expand the **Walkthroughs** node and select the name of the walkthrough.
2. Click on the edge of the crop region.
3. In the *Modify | Cameras* tab>Walkthrough panel, click

    (Edit Walkthrough).
4. The *Edit Walkthrough* tab displays additional tools and the Options Bar displays the location controls, as shown in Figure B–18.

Figure B–18

5. Set the *Frame* number to **1**.

6. In the *Edit Walkthrough* tab>Walkthrough panel, click

    (Play).

Modifying a Walkthrough

When you are modifying a walkthrough, it can help to have both the walkthrough view and the plan view open at the same time. This enables you to see the 3D view and modify the path in the 2D view.

Controls	With the plan view active, select either **Active Camera**, **Path**, **Add Key Frame**, or **Remove Key Frame**. Then, modify the controls.
Frame #	Moves the cursor to the specified frame.
Arrow buttons	Use when you are viewing the walkthrough to ensure that it displays the views you are expecting. You can select from ◁◁ (Previous Key Frame), ◁‖ (Previous Frame), ‖▷ (Next Frame), ▷▷‖ (Next Key Frame), and ▷ (Play). To stop playing, press \<Esc\> or click **Cancel** in the Status Bar.
👣	**Open Walkthrough** opens the specified frame. Modify the crop window in one frame, it modifies in all frames.
📷	**Reset Cameras.** If you move the direction of the camera in a frame, clicking this button to reset all of the changed camera directions to the original path.

- If you click in a view while editing a walkthrough, an alert box opens, prompting you to decide whether to continue editing the walkthrough.

Setting Walkthrough Frames

To upgrade the performance of the walkthrough and smooth out portions where the rate of change appears to be too fast, you can change the number of frames between key frames.

In Properties, scroll down to the *Other* section and click the button next to the *Walkthrough Frames* parameter, as shown in Figure B–19.

The button displays the number of frames in the walkthrough.

Figure B–19

7. In the Walkthrough Frames dialog box (shown in Figure B–20), you can adjust the frame number, increment, or travel per frame. Clear the **Uniform Speed** option to change individual frame times.

Walkthrough Frames

| Total Frames : | 300 | | Total Time : | 20 |

☑ Uniform Speed   Frames per second : 15

KeyFrame	Frame	Accelerator	Speed (per sec)	Elapsed Time (sec)
1	1.0	1.0	8340 mm	0.1
2	31.5	1.0	8340 mm	2.1
3	64.8	1.0	8340 mm	4.3
4	96.8	1.0	8340 mm	6.5
5	137.5	1.0	8340 mm	9.2
6	174.2	1.0	8340 mm	11.6
7	214.4	1.0	8340 mm	14.3
8	236.4	1.0	8340 mm	15.8
9	251.5	1.0	8340 mm	16.8

☐ Indicators

Frame increment : 5

| OK | Cancel | Apply | Help |

Figure B–20

How To: Export a Walkthrough

To show the walkthrough outside the Autodesk Revit software, you need to create an AVI file.

1. Open the walkthrough.

2. In the *File* tab, click (Export)> (Images and Animations)> (Walkthrough).

3. Fill out the Length/Format dialog box, as shown in Figure B–21. In the *Output Length* area, specify which frames you want to include and the number of frames per second. In the *Format* area, select how you want the movie to display. You can display in **Wireframe**, **Hidden Line**, **Shaded**, **Shaded with Edges**, **Consistent Color**, **Realistic**, **Realistic with Edges**, and **Rendering**. Use the existing dimensions or specify a zoom scale factor.

Autodesk Raytracer settings are used if you are in the Rendering display.

Figure B–21

4. Click **OK**
5. In the Export Walkthrough dialog box, specify the folder and name for the new file.
6. Click **Save**.
7. In the Video Compression dialog box, select the format and quality and click **OK**. The walkthrough displays as it creates the video file.

• You need significant computer resources (CPU and RAM) to produce AVI files.

Practice B1 | Create Walkthroughs

Practice Objective

- Create an interior walkthrough and edit it to display better views along the path.

In this practice, you will create a walkthrough in a building, as shown in plan view in Figure B–22.

Figure B–22

Task 1 - Create an interior walkthrough.

1. In the practice files folder, open **Midrise-Walkthrough-M.rvt**.

2. Open the **Floor Plans: Level 1** view.

3. In the *View* tab>Create panel (or Quick Access Toolbar), expand (3D View) and click (Walkthrough).

4. Select points to create a path that comes in through the front entrance, then goes to the left side into the reception room and conference room, in which the furniture and ceilings have been configured.

5. After the last point, click (Finish Walkthrough).

Task 2 - Test and edit the walkthrough.

1. Open the **Walkthroughs: Walkthrough1** view and the **Floor Plans: Level 1** view. Tile these two views.

2. In the walkthrough view, select the edge of the crop region.

3. In the *Modify | Cameras* tab>Walkthrough panel, click (Edit Walkthrough).

4. In the Options Bar, set the *Frame* to **1**.

5. Return to the *Edit Walkthrough* tab>Walkthrough panel, click (Play).

6. Edit the walkthrough as needed. Adjust the camera at different frames or speed up the process through some turns.

7. If you have time and computer resources, create an AVI file of your walkthrough.

Command Summary

Button	Command	Location
Materials		
	Materials	• **Ribbon:** *Manage* tab>Settings panel
	Paint	• **Ribbon:** *Manage* tab>Settings panel
Walkthroughs		
	Edit Walkthrough	• **Ribbon:** *Modify	Cameras* tab> Walkthrough panel
	Export Walkthrough	• **Ribbon:** *File* tab> Export> Images & Animations>Walkthrough
	Open Walkthrough	• **Ribbon:** *Edit Walkthrough* tab> Walkthrough panel
	Walkthrough	• **Ribbon:** *View* tab>Create panel, expand 3D View • **Quick Access Toolbar:** expand 3D View

Index

www.ingramcontent.com/pod-product-compliance
Lightning Source LLC
LaVergne TN
LVHW062313060326
832902LV00013B/2186